The Soccer Goalkeeper

Third Edition

Joseph A. Luxbacher, PhD

Gene Klein, MEd

Human Kinetics

Library of Congress Cataloging-in-Publication Data

Luxbacher, Joe.
    The soccer goalkeeper / Joseph A. Luxbacher, Gene Klein.-- 3rd ed.
        p. cm.
Includes index.
    ISBN 0-7360-4180-X (soft cover)
    1. Soccer--Goalkeeping.   I. Klein, Gene. II. Title.
    GV943.9.G62 L88 2002
    796.334'26--dc21

                                                  2002006856

ISBN: 0-7360-4180-X

Developmental Editor: Leigh LaHood
Copyeditor: John Wentworth
Proofreader: Sarah Wiseman
Indexer: Betty Frizzéll
Graphic Designer and Graphic Artist: Judy Henderson
Photo Manager: Leslie A. Woodrum
Cover Designer: Keith Blomberg
Photographer (cover): Brian Bahr/Allsport
Photographer (interior): Leslie A. Woodrum, unless otherwise noted
Art Manager: Carl D. Johnson
Illustrator: Roberto Sabas
Printer: United Graphics

Human Kinetics books are available at special discounts for bulk purchase. Special editions or book excerpts can also be created to specification. For details, contact the Special Sales Manager at Human Kinetics.

Printed in the United States of America   10   9   8   7   6   5   4   3   2   1

Human Kinetics
Web site: www.HumanKinetics.com

United States: Human Kinetics
P.O. Box 5076
Champaign, IL 61825-5076
800-747-4457
e-mail: humank@hkusa.com

Canada: Human Kinetics
475 Devonshire Road Unit 100
Windsor, ON N8Y 2L5
800-465-7301 (in Canada only)
e-mail: orders@hkcanada.com

Europe: Human Kinetics
107 Bradford Road
Stanningly
Leeds LS28 6AT, United Kingdom
+44 (0) 113 255 5665
e-mail: hk@hkeurope.com

Australia: Human Kinetics
57A Price Avenue
Lower Mitcham, South Australia 5062
08 8277 1555
e-mail: liahka@senet.com.au

New Zealand: Human Kinetics
P.O. Box 105-231, Auckland Central
09-523-3462
e-mail: hkp@ihug.co.nz

To aspiring goalkeepers everywhere

Contents

Foreword

I played goalkeeper in England's professional league for 19 years and have spent the past 20 years coaching soccer in the United States, with a primary focus on goalkeeper development. In my present role as a U.S. Soccer national staff coach, I am responsible for developing the goalkeepers in our Olympic Development and National Team programs and also establishing a goalkeeper coaching education program that will help both goalies and coaches better understand this "mysterious" position on the team.

Because of my position and background, goalkeepers and coaches often ask me to recommend a good publication that explains and shows specific goalkeeper drills that are realistic to game situations. This third edition of *The Soccer Goalkeeper* by Joe Luxbacher and Gene Klein is such a book; I am very impressed with its content.

The material is presented in an excellent format for male and female goalkeepers to learn from and use. The text and illustrations break down individual techniques so that the goalkeeper or coach can readily grasp them. Mastering these fundamentals will provide a foundation on which goalies can build their game. The content progresses from the basics through to game situations.

A main feature of the book is the abundant drills available for goalkeepers and coaches to use in practice sessions to master almost every goalkeeping skill. The work also illustrates and explains how to develop specific areas of goalkeeping expertise, presenting situations a goalkeeper is most likely to experience during a game and how to best handle them. The drills progress to a tactical, team level where the goalkeeper must execute techniques proficiently and make tactical decisions in a split second in order to be successful. Repetition of such drills helps to develop the goalkeeper's mental focus and toughness to meet the great demands of the goalkeeper position.

My many years as a goalkeeper coach have taught me that training should be as straightforward and realistic to the game as possible. The four components of goalkeeper performance—technical, tactical, psychological, and physical—are presented in a clear and functional manner in *The Soccer Goalkeeper*. It was a pleasure to read and I highly recommend that you do so.

Peter Mellor
United States Soccer Federation
National Teams Staff Goalkeeper Coach and Co-coordinator

Preface

The game of soccer is in a state of perpetual change. Systems of play, methods of coaching, player roles and responsibilities, and philosophies of training are constantly evolving in an ongoing effort to maximize individual and team performance. In the midst of these changes stands the soccer goalkeeper, the player whose primary responsibility remains as it has always been—to keep the ball out of the back of the net. To meet that challenge successfully requires a special type of athlete. The goalkeeper must partner a high degree of mental toughness with outstanding physical ability. Strength, speed off the mark, quickness, flexibility, and mobility are essential physical assets. Mastery of fundamental footwork is required to set the stage for proper execution of the techniques used when receiving low, medium, and high balls, diving to save, boxing the high ball, and smothering the breakaway, to name just a few. To truly excel, the goalkeeper must go one step further. Coupled with outstanding physical skills must be a working knowledge of how and when to implement those skills within the framework of team play. A clear understanding of angle play and positional responsibilities, how to organize the defense, and how and when to initiate team attacks enables an aspiring goalkeeper to elevate performance to the next level.

As the saying so aptly states, you usually get what you earn in life. Becoming a top-flight goalkeeper does not occur by chance—the right must be earned. Toward that aim, the importance of thorough preparation and proper training cannot be overstated. Almost 10 years have passed since publication of the second edition of *The Soccer Goalkeeper*. During that span several rule changes have been implemented that restrict the goalkeeper from using the hands in certain situations. The keeper can no longer handle a ball that has been deliberately passed back to him or her from a teammate or a ball arriving directly from a throw-in. These changes require modern keepers to be more adept than their predecessors at using their feet to control and distribute the ball. Today's goalkeepers must also be prepared to play a more prominent role in team attack. The third edition of *The Soccer Goalkeeper* addresses the ever-expanding role of the goalkeeper and provides essential information to enable the keeper to achieve maximum performance in matches. New and improved illustrations and high-quality demonstration photos clarify proper execution of essential goalkeeper skills. Expanded drill sections at the end of each chapter provide up-to-date training exercises to develop goalkeepers of various ages and ability levels. Greater emphasis has been placed on the fundamental footwork used to maximize coverage of the goal and penalty areas. A new chapter is devoted entirely to the keeper's important role in initiating team attack once the save has been made.

In short, the third edition of *The Soccer Goalkeeper* is the most comprehensive, well-organized, in-depth discussion of the goalkeeper position available today. Players and coaches can take the material provided in this book and incorporate it directly into their training programs. When doing so, they should keep in mind that even the most up-to-date information and best training exercises can take a team or individual only so far. Thorough mastery of goalkeeper skills and a complete understanding of how to play the position can be achieved only through hard work and dedicated practice. Coaches and the goalkeepers under their charge should work together to realize that objective. Coaches are responsible for providing an optimal training environment, one that prepares the goalkeeper to successfully meet the physical and mental challenges encountered in the game. The goalkeeper must supply the commitment, work ethic, motivation, and discipline needed to maximize his or her abilities. Only through coaches and goalkeepers working in concert can individual and team performance be elevated to a new level, a level truly deserving of the number one player on the soccer field.

Acknowledgments

The writing and publishing of a book truly requires a team effort. In that regard the authors are greatly indebted to a number of people for their generous help and support. Although it is not possible to list everyone by name, we would like to extend our sincere gratitude to the following individuals: to Leigh LaHood, Ted Miller, Les Woodrum, and the staff at Human Kinetics for their expertise and professional approach to the project; to Peter Mellor, U.S. National Team Staff Goalkeeper Coach and Co-coordinator, for his willingness to provide the foreword; to Kelme USA and Sondico for providing the goalkeeper equipment used in the skill demonstration photos; to goalkeepers Rachel Brown, Joe Conlan, Randy Dedini (Pittsburgh Riverhounds), Justin Gaul, and Justin Lowery, for their willingness to model the skills and techniques portrayed in the demonstration photos.

Special thanks go to our wives and children for their encouragement and patience throughout the writing process. Finally, we extend our sincere appreciation to the many fine players, coaches, and colleagues who contributed to our efforts through their willingness to share thoughts and ideas.

Key to Diagrams

GK	Goalkeeper
X	Field player; attacker
O	Field player; defender
⊗	Neutral player or flank player
S	Server
Coach	Coach
- - - -▶	Path of ball
───▶	Path of player
∿∿∿▶	Dribble
- - - -▶	Shot

Equipping the Body for Action

Top-flight goalkeepers share common physical attributes. Most are tall and rangy and possess excellent jumping ability. A high degree of agility, balance, and body control enable them to react suddenly to rapidly changing situations that occur in the goalmouth. Above average levels of muscular strength and power enable them to catch and control powerful shots and crosses and, when necessary, to fend off the determined challenge of opponents attempting to win the ball. Powerful legs enable them to leap up and over teammates and opponents to collect high balls lofted into the goal area. Last but certainly not least, elite goalkeepers demonstrate an ability to catch and hold even the most difficult of shots. They rarely give up rebounds once they get their hands on the ball. That being said, lacking one or more of the aforementioned qualities does not necessarily preclude someone from developing into an outstanding keeper. Ability to execute the various goalkeeper skills as well as intangible qualities such as mental toughness, competitiveness, and an unyielding determination to succeed also play important roles in being an outstanding keeper. That said, a high degree of athleticism and physical prowess provide the foundation for optimal goalkeeper performance.

In addition to being physically and mentally prepared to play the position, a goalkeeper must also dress for success. The keeper usually sports a bright-colored jersey different from that of teammates. Unlike the standard uniform worn by field players, the goalkeeper's uniform has light padding sewn into the jersey and pants to soften collisions with the ground or opposing players when diving to make a save. A detailed discussion of goalkeeper equipment appears later in this chapter.

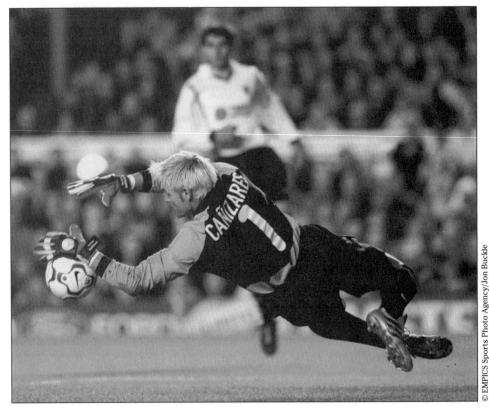

Top goalkeepers demonstrate the ability to catch and hold the most difficult shots.

Physical Attributes

An old coaching adage states, "great athletes are born, not made." This is partly true. All of us inherit physical attributes from our parents—heart and lung size, muscle fiber characteristics, skeletal structure, body type, and so on—that impose limits on our potential for physical development. Most players never come anywhere close to reaching their physical limits, however, so if aspiring goalkeepers are lacking one or more of the desired inherited attributes, they can usually compensate by fully developing attributes that can be gained through hard work and proper training. While it's not possible to change your genes, you can change your habits. Developing good training habits enables you to become the best goalkeeper you can be—which is probably pretty good.

Height

All other things being equal, a tall goalkeeper usually has an edge over a shorter keeper when attempting to cover 192 square feet of goal. Thankfully, in the real world, all other things aren't equal. For example, a shorter goalkeeper can compensate for lack of height by developing excellent catching and receiving skills, improving jumping ability through enhanced leg strength and power, positioning at the proper angle with the ball and distance off of the goal line, and reading the game and correctly anticipating the actions and intentions of opponents.

Strength

To be a great shot-saver the goalkeeper must be able to respond quickly with power, balance, and body control in virtually any situation. Strong arms, shoulders, and chest are required to catch and hold powerfully driven shots and crosses into the goal area and to distribute the ball over long distances by throwing. Powerful legs propel the keeper up and over opponents to collect the high ball and to distribute the ball over long distances by punting or drop-kicking. *Functional strength*—that is, strength specific to the movements regularly performed in defense of the goal—is more important for a goalkeeper than *absolute strength* (e.g., how much weight can be lifted at one time). With that in mind, goalkeeper-conditioning activities should whenever possible mirror the physical demands encountered in actual match situations. Muscular strength and endurance can be improved through the use of free-weight exercises, exercise weight machines, and manual resistance exercises.

Power

Muscular power, by definition, is the product of strength and speed of movement. Power is the explosive aspect of strength and provides a measure of how quickly someone can display strength through a range of motion. For the soccer goalkeeper, muscular power is more important than pure strength. Movements such as leaping above an opponent to intercept a crossed ball and vaulting sideways with body fully extended to save a driven shot depend, in large part, on an adequate level of muscular power. Muscular power can be developed through soccer-specific weight training coupled with plyometric exercises.

Soft Hands

Although large hands may provide a slight advantage over smaller hands when attempting to catch a ball, hand size is not all that significant to the goalkeeper. Of greater importance is the ability to receive and hold even the most difficult shots. Coaches refer to this attribute as having "soft hands." Hands of stone might be desirable if you want to make your mark in the sport of boxing, but they don't serve well in defense of the goal.

The goalkeeper can develop soft hands through repetitive practice of fundamental catching techniques. Ball-handling exercises are provided in chapter 3.

Flexibility

Flexibility is the range of possible movement around a joint or series of joints. Poor flexibility diminishes the ability to perform a number of essential goalkeeper skills and may also increase the likelihood of muscle pulls and connective tissue injury. Although range of motion around certain joints is limited by factors out of our control (e.g., bony structure), in most areas of the body we can improve flexibility through a comprehensive program of stretching exercises.

Historically, two forms of stretching have been popular with coaches and trainers. *Ballistic stretching* involves bobbing movements that gradually extend the muscle(s) to increasingly greater lengths. The alternative method is called *static stretching*. Rather than using bouncing movements to stretch the muscle, static stretches slowly extend the target muscle(s) to its greatest possible length without discomfort. The stretch position is held for 15 to 30 seconds before being slowly released and is then repeated for another 15 to 30 seconds. Although both types of stretching exercises improve range of motion, sport scientists generally agree that static stretches are preferable because they do not subject the muscles to the sudden pressures of bouncing movements. Slow and steady extension of the target muscles also prevents firing of the stretch reflex, the body's natural safeguard against muscles extending beyond their limits. For best results, stretch every day or at least every other day. Keep in mind that people vary greatly in range of motion, so stretching should never become a competition among teammates. Measure your progress against your own standards and initial state of flexibility.

Agility

Agility is a measure of the ability to change direction rapidly without losing balance or speed—clearly a critical element affecting a goalkeeper's ability to react quickly when saving a deflected shot or misdirected cross into the goal. A player's level of agility depends on several fitness factors, including strength, power, balance, speed, coordination, and flexibility. Goalkeepers can improve agility through game-related training activities that incorporate sudden changes of speed and direction coupled with proper footwork. Because agility gradually diminishes with the onset of physical fatigue, the keeper should develop a high level of muscular strength and endurance. A fatigued goalkeeper is likely to be an error-prone goalkeeper.

Agility is a crucial skill for a goalkeeper to master.

Footwork

Proper footwork is directly linked to the goalkeeper's level of mobility and agility. The ability to execute the foot movements appropriate for a specific game situation enables the keeper to cover the largest possible area of the goal and penalty areas, allowing him or her to position to best advantage. Common foot movements include the side shuffle, collapse step, power step, drop step, drop step/crossover step, crossover sprint, backpedal, and vertical jump. Chapter 8 provides an in-depth description of each technique and when to use it in game situations. Drills are also provided to improve the keeper's ability to perform these essential foot movements.

Tools of the Trade

While a high degree of athleticism is undoubtedly the most essential piece of the performance puzzle, it is not the only piece. For goalkeepers to consistently perform at a high level they must be properly equipped with the fundamental "tools of the trade." The keeper requires a set of equipment different from that of field players. The basic goalkeeper uniform includes a jersey, shorts or pants, socks, shin guards, shoes, and gloves.

Goalkeeper Jersey

The traditional goalkeeper jersey is long-sleeved with thin layers of padding at the elbows, shoulders, and chest (figure 1.1). Short-sleeved jerseys have become more popular in recent years primarily because they are lighter and less restrictive. The tradeoff is that short-sleeved shirts provide less padding and protection than long-sleeved models do. Federation Internationale de Football Association (FIFA) rules specify that the goalkeeper's jersey must differ in color from that of the field players.

Figure 1.1 A typical goalkeeper jersey.

Most keepers wear bright, multicolored jerseys to clearly distinguish themselves from teammates and opponents. Wearing a bright-colored jersey may also provide an advantage for the keeper. It's possible that opponents under pressure to quickly release a shot instinctively kick toward the brightest spot in their immediate field of vision—the keeper's jersey.

Goalkeeper jerseys are typically more expensive than those field players wear. Prices range from $50 to more than $100 depending on the quality. To avoid color conflicts with opponents, the keeper should bring two or three jerseys to each game. An extra jersey might also come in handy in the event of rain or muddy field conditions.

Goalkeeper Shorts or Pants

Most keepers prefer to wear knee-length shorts that cover the upper thigh and hamstrings (figure 1.2). Typically, shorts are made of nylon or a polyester/cotton blend and have thin padding over the hips to protect against bruises. Full-length pants with thin padding around the hips and over the knees are also available. Full-length models are commonly worn when training or playing on artificial turf or hard, dry natural surfaces. Long pants are a must when playing indoor soccer.

Figure 1.2 Goalkeeper shorts.

Socks and Shin Guards

Goalkeepers wear the same style sock as field players do, but their socks are usually a different color. The most popular sock is the full-footed model that can be pulled up to just below the knee. Shin guards are secured underneath the sock to protect against lower leg injuries that can result from collisions when attempting to block a shot or smother a loose ball in the goal area. Shin guards cover the front area of the leg between the ankle and the knee. Most models are made of light, semiflexible plastic and are inexpensive.

Shoes

Although the goalkeeper does not run nearly as far or as fast as the field players during the course of a game, solid footing is a prerequisite for successful performance. The quick movements and sudden changes of direction required when reacting to a shot or cross cannot be performed without solid traction. Four general categories of soccer shoes are available—screw-ins, molded, turf, and flats—that differ primarily in the type of sole. Screw-in studded soles are the best choice when playing on thick grass or on wet and soggy surfaces. Most shoes have six or eight medium-length cleats, or studs, that can be replaced when damaged or worn. Screw-ins are not appropriate for use on hard natural field surfaces or artificial turf. Molded-sole shoes have a dozen or more short- to medium-length rubber spikes that give adequate traction on virtually all types of field surfaces. The spikes are not removable. Turf shoes are generally worn on artificial surfaces but are also appropriate for hard, dry natural surfaces. The soles are composed of short, pebble-type cleats that provide maximum traction on hard surfaces. Turf shoes are somewhat heavier and less flexible than screw-ins or molded-sole shoes and are not the first choice of most soccer players. Flats are designed for indoor soccer played on artificial surfaces. They are lighter in weight than turf shoes and can also be worn on dry, hard outdoor surfaces.

When selecting a shoe, take into account cost, comfort, durability, and versatility. Although a higher price does not guarantee a better shoe, you usually get what you pay for. Top-of-the-line screw-ins are the shoe of choice for most college and professional players. They are also more expensive than other types of shoes, costing well over $100 a pair.

Gloves

Gloves have become an essential part of the goalkeeper's equipment. In years past, goalkeepers wore gloves only in the most inclement weather conditions to improve their grip on the ball. Today's keepers wear specialized gloves in even ideal field and weather conditions. Rarely if ever will you see a professional keeper without gloves. Most models are made of soft, thin leather with a foam-rubber palm. Velcro wrist straps secure the gloves tightly to the hands and wrists (figure 1.3). Most keepers prefer to wear gloves slightly larger than their hands, as the increased surface area makes it easier to hold the ball and allows the glove longer wear. Goalkeeper gloves come in many styles and models, so prices vary. Expect to pay between $50 and $150 for a quality pair of gloves.

Optional Equipment

A variety of optional equipment is available. Some keepers like to wear thin nylon shorts underneath their regular goalkeeper pants. The shorts help prevent scrapes and abrasions that can occur through repeated sliding and diving during training sessions. Younger keepers who lack proper diving technique will sometimes wear elbow and knee pads during training sessions to limit bumps and bruises. Pads are somewhat bulky and can restrict range of movement, so they are not recommended for game competition. A cap or visor can be worn on days when a bright sun high in the sky impairs the keeper's ability to follow the ball. Before wearing a hat in game competition, the keeper should become accustomed to the hat by wearing it during practice. Finally, young goalkeepers sometimes wear protective head gear to reduce the risk of head injury. Helmets are lightweight and made of hard rubber or plastic. The use of head gear is

Figure 1.3 Gloves.

more common in indoor soccer, where space is restricted and collisions in the goal area are more likely.

Preparing for Success

A keeper does not become top-notch by chance. Thorough preparation and a commitment to excellence are key to optimal performance in the goal. To consistently perform at a high level of play, goalkeepers must physically prepare their bodies to meet the demands of the position. A rigorous conditioning program can improve muscular strength, power, endurance, and flexibility. Developing proper ball-handling techniques enhances the ability to hold the most difficult of shots. Wearing appropriate equipment for game situations—shoes that provide good traction, gloves that aid in holding a slippery ball, a visor that blocks out a blinding sun—provide the best chance for success. Keepers who prepare to the fullest increase their self-confidence, which in turn improves their mental approach to the game, as discussed in chapter 2.

Developing Mental Skills

From a psychological point of view, the goalkeeper occupies what is arguably the most difficult of team positions. Although each member of the team must accept responsibility for any physical and mental errors committed during the heat of competition, mistakes by the keeper are generally punished immediately and more severely than those of field players. Simply put, a mistake by the goalkeeper most often results in a goal scored against the team. It is not a position for the faint of heart or weak of spirit. To consistently perform at a high level requires outstanding physical tools coupled with a high degree of mental toughness.

There is much truth to the old coaching adage "where the mind goes, the body will follow." Your mental approach to the game largely determines your ability to succeed in pressure situations and to psychologically overcome mistakes committed by yourself or teammates. To win the mental game, every keeper must master the three Cs of goalkeeping: courage, concentration, and confidence.

Courage

Action in and around the goal area is usually fast, furious, and physical. Goalkeepers must expect to be involved in physical challenges during a match. They may have to dive at the feet of an onrushing opponent to smother a loose ball. They might need to sacrifice their body to block a point-blank shot. Basically, keepers have to do whatever it takes to keep the ball out of the back of the net. Given the fact that a moment's hesitation to act or single error in judgment can cost a team the game, a high degree of mental toughness is extremely important for the goalkeeper. Keepers must be prepared to make split-second decisions in the heat of competition and be able to deal with the consequences of their actions. When errors in judgment do occur—and invariably they will for every goalkeeper at one time or another—keepers must not allow them to affect their confidence or concentration. They need to put the mistake behind them and move on immediately. An important lesson all great athletes learn at one point or another is that the last play should not affect the next play. This lesson is particularly crucial for the soccer goalkeeper.

Concentration

The ability to focus on the task at hand, to filter out distractions that can impair judgment, is essential for a goalkeeper. Even worse than physical errors, mental errors committed by the goalkeeper have a depressing effect on the psychological state of the team. The keeper must be physically and mentally ready to make the big save, whether it's in the first or final minute of play. Doing so requires a constant state of readiness, from opening kickoff to final whistle. A keeper must direct total attention to

© Bongarts Photography/Henri Szwarc

Goalkeepers must be physically and mentally prepared to deal with fast and furious action around the net.

the immediate situation. The likelihood of committing a mental error is heightened if the keeper looks back to a previous play or looks beyond the next play.

A good keeper deals immediately and effectively with adversity, including the ultimate frustration and embarrassment associated with a "bad" goal. Dwell on a mistake, and you'll likely make another one. The ability to get past errors quickly is the important psychological tool that enables a keeper to mentally prepare for the next shot, to make the next save. Self-assessment of performance should be conducted after the match, not during the heat of competition.

Mental Preparation

With the unique nature of their position, goalkeepers are the only true specialists on the field. In one respect, however, goalkeepers are just like field players—they come to the team with unique personalities and motivations. So it's not possible to prescribe a single method of pregame mental preparation that guarantees an optimal state of readiness. What works for one keeper might not work for another. It's best for keepers to follow their instincts, learn from past experiences, and use motivational techniques that work best for them. The following material can be adapted to meet a variety of circumstances.

Prematch Preparation

Maintaining focus through a 90-minute match is a difficult task, particularly for younger players with limited attention spans. Even experienced keepers sometimes fall prey to momentary lapses in concentration during games in which they handle the ball infrequently. To keep this from happening, mental preparation for the upcoming match should begin shortly after the most recent match has ended. An assessment of the keeper's performance during the previous game should provide a reasonably accurate measure of current strengths and weaknesses. Identify those elements of the game (speed of decision making, focus, assertiveness) that could use improvement and make those aspects the primary emphasis of training sessions. The old coaching adage "you play like you practice" still holds true. High-intensity training in competitive game-simulated situations improves confidence and the ability to make split-second decisions under stressful situations. As a result, the keeper becomes mentally and physically tougher.

Prematch preparation should also include a thorough analysis of the upcoming opponent. What is the team's style of play? Do they channel their attack through the center or attempt to spread the field and attack from the flanks? Who are their most dangerous attacking players? What are their tendencies on free kick plays? Are corner kicks in-swingers or out-swingers? Answers to these and other questions prepare keepers for what they might face in the game. Efforts to gain a mental edge should continue right up until game time. Prior to the match, inspect the field surface and, in particular, the goal and penalty areas. Note the position of the sun and the path it will follow during the course of the game. Take into account the effect that wind or rain may have on efforts to distribute the ball, and choose the most appropriate technique. Consider other factors that might affect play. The more acclimated the keeper is to the specific game environment, the more comfortable he or she feels, and the easier it is to focus on the game. Last but not least, a rigorous warm-up prior to kickoff will heighten focus and get you mentally ready to perform your best.

Maintaining Focus During the Match

Soccer is a game of improvisation, spontaneous and for the most part unrehearsed. The play can be highly unpredictable, so the keeper must be totally immersed in action from the opening whistle. He or she should try to experience every pass and feel every tackle, to anticipate every action of the opposing team. A conscious effort must be made to block out potential distractions—poor field surface, inclement weather, verbally abusive spectators—that could disrupt concentration. Keepers should focus on elements of play that might give them a performance edge, such as position of the ball, movement of opponents, and organizing the defense.

- **Position of the ball.** The ball should be kept in vision at all times. The keeper must maintain an optimal state of readiness when opponents have possession of the ball within striking distance of the goal.
- **Movement of opponents.** The keeper should be aware of opponents stationed in and around the penalty area, anticipating their movements and positions.
- **Organizing the defense.** From a vantage point behind the last line of defenders, the keeper is in an excellent position to see the entire field and anticipate how the play will develop. A good keeper verbally communicates information to teammates so that they can position properly with respect to the ball and opponents. Commands should be loud and straightforward.

Confidence

Confidence is a state of mind that frees a person to perform at the highest level possible. It is the key that opens the door to realizing full potential. Coaches understand that as confidence improves, athletes become more

From the opening whistle to the end of the game, top goalkeepers like Fabien Barthez of Manchester United and France are immersed in every action on the field.

consistent performers. Confidence enables a player to relax in critical game situations. Performance is enhanced because focus remains laser sharp, even during the most difficult of times. In this respect, the elements of confidence, mental focus, and athletic performance are interdependent and closely linked.

Developing a high degree of confidence takes time and effort. True confidence is developed through an ongoing commitment to mental and physical preparation. Goalkeepers should strive to learn from every situation experienced in the goal, the good and the bad. They should keep a mental record of best days and best performances. They should focus on their strengths but be realistic enough to recognize their limitations and work to improve them. In this way confidence grows, as the keeper realizes he or she is learning and improving with each experience. Support from coaches and teammates can also play a vital role. When those closest to the keeper express true confidence in his or her abilities, it has a positive effect on the whole team. When teammates are confident that the goalkeeper will do the job, they can focus fully on their own roles and responsibilities. In this way the whole becomes greater than the sum of its parts.

So how does a keeper gain the confidence and trust of teammates? There's only one surefire way we know of—earn it! A tough mental attitude and solid work ethic during training sessions are essential. Demonstrating superior performance in match competition doesn't hurt either. But there are other ways to subtly instill confidence in teammates as well.

• **Dominate the box.** The penalty box is the goalkeeper's personal kingdom, and everyone in the park should be made aware of it. The keeper should be aggressive and assertive in defense of the goal.

• **Organize the defense.** A good keeper does not hesitate to issue verbal commands to teammates. From a position behind the defense, the keeper has a more complete view of the field than they do, and better perception of what the opponents are trying to do. We're not talking meaningless chatter or cheerleading, but if something needs saying, the keeper needs to speak up and say it with force. Teammates will value and respect a loud, clear voice of authority.

• **Demand the ball.** Clearly, the opposing team cannot score when the goalkeeper has possession of the ball. Keepers should be active and aggressive within the penalty area, attempting to field any shot or cross within their reach. They should demonstrate through actions as well as words that they want to handle the ball.

• **Psych out opponents.** Some keepers like to do their pregame warm-up in full view of the opposing team, using quick-reaction saves and acrobatic dives to intimidate opponents and boost their own confidence. In some cases such gamesmanship has the desired effect, and at other times it might not. Here's an example. We were fortunate enough to attend the 1986 World Cup final played between Germany and Argentina in Azteca Stadium in Mexico. About 40 minutes before the kickoff, German international Tony Schumacher, one of the most physically intimidating goalkeepers of the modern era, entered the stadium alone and conducted his pregame warm-up in the center of the field. More than 120,000 spectators, as well as the entire Argentine team, watched Schumacher go through a routine obviously designed to psych himself up and intimidate his opponents. While the routine might have had the desired effect on Schumacher, the Argentine team was not intimidated. They put three goals past Schumacher in 90 minutes of regulation time to claim the world title.

Setting Your Own Limits

Although the support of teammates, coaches, and significant others is helpful to the positive development of a goalkeeper, a keeper must accept that he or she alone is responsible for creating the state of mind needed to excel. A commitment to excellence is ultimately self-generated and self-directed. Many athletes never come to this realization, and as a result they never fulfill their potential. They blame personal shortcomings on the decisions of a coach or the actions of teammates. This is a losing mindset. Developing keepers need to accept responsibility for becoming better and better. No one else—not parents, coaches, or teammates—can make the commitment for them. It comes from within. The ultimate question a keeper must ask is, *Am I truly prepared to make the commitment?* If the answer is yes, then the first and most important step has been taken in the process of becoming the best goalkeeper possible.

Receiving Low and Medium-Height Balls

The goalkeeper should be prepared to handle shots arriving at various angles and velocities. Although some saves are by necessity acrobatic and spectacular in nature, the majority require routine execution of fundamental goalkeeper techniques. In all cases, the keeper must demonstrate two critical skills: (1) the ability to move quickly in any direction and (2) the ability to receive and hold the ball.

The ability to react quickly in a variety of situations requires the keeper to maintain balance and body control at all times. All movements begin with the keeper positioned in the standard goalkeeper posture, commonly called the "ready" position. To receive a low or medium-height ball, the keeper should quickly move to a position between the goal and the oncoming ball. Once positioned, the next step is to field the ball cleanly. In all cases, the overriding objective is to secure the ball and avoid rebounds. To accomplish this, the keeper must be fundamentally sound in the techniques used to receive balls traveling along the ground as well as those arriving through the air.

Basic Goalkeeper Stance

Assume the ready position (figure 3.1) whenever an opponent with the ball is within scoring distance of the goal. Face the ball with shoulders square and feet positioned approximately shoulder-width apart. Lean forward slightly with body weight centered over the balls of the feet. Keep the upper body erect, with knees flexed. Position hips and buttocks as if sitting on a medium-height stool. Carry hands at approximately waist level with forearms parallel to the ground and palms facing forward. Hands and fingers should be relaxed. It's important to get set in the ready position prior to the shot, as it's difficult to maintain proper balance and body control if you're shifting at the moment the shot is released. Experienced keepers make it a practice to set the feet early with head steady and vision focused on the ball.

Figure 3.1 Two styles of the ready position: (a) standing stance, and (b) lower posture, "gorilla stance."

The Ready Position

1. Square shoulders with ball.
2. Maintain balance and body control.
3. Center weight forward over balls of feet.
4. Flex knees slightly for maximum stability.
5. Keep head and upper body steady.
6. Set feet at the instant the shot is released.

Low (Ground) Balls

We'll define a low ball as a shot directed toward the goal that is arriving at ground level. A low ball can be either rolling or skimming along the ground surface. To receive the ball, the keeper has the option of several techniques, depending on the nature of the shot. A ball rolling directly at the keeper is received in a different manner from a ball arriving to the side. Similarly, a powerfully driven ball skimming along the ground poses a more difficult challenge for the keeper than a slow roller and is received using a different technique.

Receiving a Rolling Ball

Making routine plays consistently is more important than pulling off a spectacular save once in a while. A large percentage of goalkeeper saves involve rolling balls. Two different techniques—the standing save and the kneeling save—are used to receive a rolling ball, depending on the velocity of the shot and if the ball's coming directly at the keeper or to the side.

The Standing Save

A ball rolling directly at the keeper is received using the "scoop" technique. In this technique, the keeper faces the ball with shoulders square, legs straight, and feet positioned a few inches apart. As the ball arrives, the keeper bends forward at the waist with arms extended down. Palms face forward and are slightly cupped with fingers pointed toward the ball. Fingertips should be at ground level and forearms parallel to one another. The keeper does not attempt to catch the rolling ball directly in the hands. Instead, he or she slips hands underneath and allows the ball to roll up onto the wrists and forearms (figure 3.2a). The keeper then immediately returns to an upright position with the ball clutched securely against the chest (figure 3.2b).

Figure 3.2 The standing save: *(a)* allowing the ball to roll into the hands and *(b)* returning to an upright position.

KEY ELEMENTS OF PEAK PERFORMANCE

The Standing Save

1. Position body between ball and goal with shoulders square.
2. Bend forward at waist.
3. Extend arms down with palms facing forward and slightly cupped.
4. Allow the ball to contact palms first, then roll up onto wrists and forearms.
5. Withdraw body slightly to cushion impact.
6. Return to standing position.

The "Tweener" Save

In some instances the goalkeeper won't have enough time to reposition between the oncoming ball and the goal. This type of shot, commonly called a "tweener," is just far enough away to make the standing save impossible but not so far as to warrant a diving save. To receive the tweener, the keeper shuffles sideways toward the ball as quickly as possible, extending the lead foot in the direction he or she is moving, with the leg flexed at the knee. The keeper kneels on the trailing leg and positions it parallel to the goal line. The open space between the heel of the lead foot and the knee of the trailing leg should be only a few inches: too small for the ball to slip through. From the kneeling position, the keeper bends the upper body forward with shoulders square, slips hands underneath the ball, and allows the ball to roll up onto the wrists and forearms before clutching it to the chest (figure 3.3). This technique can also be used to block a difficult close-range shot that is bouncing, skipping, or arriving with some velocity.

KEY ELEMENTS OF PEAK PERFORMANCE

The Tweener Save

1. From the ready position, shuffle laterally across the goal.
2. Extend the lead foot toward the ball.
3. Kneel with the trailing leg parallel to the goal line.
4. Bend forward at the waist with shoulders square and head steady.
5. Extend arms with palms underneath ball and fingers extended.

Figure 3.3 The "tweener" save.

6. Allow the ball to roll onto wrists and forearms.

7. Straighten up and clutch the ball to chest.

Receiving a Low-Driven Ball

The conventional standing save is not appropriate when receiving a low, powerfully driven shot coming directly at the keeper or when receiving a ball that skips immediately in front of the keeper. This is especially true when playing on a slick field surface where the ball accelerates upon hitting standing water or wet grass. To compensate for the added velocity of the shot, the keeper should receive the ball using a forward vault technique. He or she faces the ball with shoulders square and bends forward at the waist with knees flexed and body balanced. As the ball arrives, the keeper vaults forward and down to the ground with arms extended and palms facing up. He or she then slips hands and forearms underneath the ball, allowing it to contact the wrists and forearms rather than the hands (figure 3.4a). The keeper falls forward and traps the ball between the forearms and chest with legs extended and spread behind (figure 3.4b). The keeper should not attempt to catch the low-driven ball directly in the hands.

KEY ELEMENTS OF PEAK PERFORMANCE

The Forward Vault

1. Position between the ball and goal with shoulders square.
2. Bend forward at waist with the knees flexed.
3. Vault forward and down to ground.
4. Extend both arms underneath the ball with palms facing up.
5. Allow the ball to contact the wrists first, then forearms.
6. Clutch ball between forearms and chest.
7. Extend and spread legs behind for stability.

The forward vault technique can also be used to smother a loose ball in the goal area and to receive a ball slotted through the defense and into the penalty area. To smother a slowly rolling ball, the keeper vaults forward with arms extended and palms facing down to forcefully pin the ball to the ground with both hands on top. Once the ball is secure, the keeper pulls it to his or her chest. To collect a ball that has been slotted through the defense, the keeper moves forward quickly, bending at the waist, and scoops up the ball between forearms and chest. The keeper is always prepared to vault past (to either side) an onrushing opponent attempting to beat him or her to the ball.

Figure 3.4 Forward vault: *(a)* allowing the ball to contact the wrists and forearms and *(b)* falling forward to trap the ball.

Medium-Height Balls

A shot arriving through the air between the ankles and waist is considered a medium-height ball. To receive a ball arriving at ankle height, the keeper uses a scoop technique similar to that used to receive a ball rolling directly at him or her (standing save). The keeper positions between the ball and goal with shoulders square, legs straight, and feet a few inches apart. As the ball arrives, he or she bends forward at the waist with arms extended down and palms forward. The keeper lets the ball contact the wrists before allowing it to roll up onto the forearms and securing it to the chest (figure 3.5). There should be no attempt to catch the medium-height ball directly in the hands, as this increases the risk of a rebound.

Figure 3.5 The standing save, used for an ankle- to waist-height ball.

To receive a medium-height ball arriving at waist height, the keeper bends forward at the waist with forearms parallel and hands extended down. As the ball contacts his or her forearms, the keeper jumps backward a few inches to absorb the impact. The greater the velocity of the shot, the greater the cushion required. Return to a standing position with the ball clutched securely between the forearms and chest.

KEY ELEMENTS OF PEAK PERFORMANCE

Receiving a Medium-Height Ball

1. Position in line with the oncoming ball.
2. Keep legs straight, feet a few inches apart.
3. Bend forward at the waist with arms extended down and forearms parallel.
4. Allow the ball to contact the wrists first before rolling onto forearms.
5. Withdraw your body as the ball arrives to cushion impact.
6. Secure the ball between forearms and chest.

Receiving Low and Medium Ball Drills

The fundamental techniques used to receive low and medium-height balls apply to all of the following exercises. Each drill is designed to emphasize a technique or combination of techniques. In all cases the keeper should focus on maintaining proper body shape as the ball arrives. This involves making sure the body is positioned behind the ball while the upper body angles forward over the ball. Palms and forearms slide underneath the ball so it can be secured to the chest. It's very important that the goalkeeper move forward to meet the ball rather than passively waiting for the ball to arrive.

Quality serves are required for the goalkeeper to get the most out of the drills on the next pages. The exercises are set up for the goalkeeper to make saves without going down on his or her side, so the shots (serves) must not be out of the keeper's reach. Although this restriction makes it more difficult for the field players to score goals, it ensures that the goalkeeper receives a maximum number of repetitions in this skill area.

PINGERS

Individual Exercise

Equipment   1 ball

Organization   Two goalkeepers (A and B) face each other 8 to 10 yards apart.

Procedure   Goalkeeper A volleys or "pings" the ball to Goalkeeper B's waist or leg area. Goalkeeper B repeats to Goalkeeper A. The keeper receiving the ball uses the scoop technique and receives the ball with palms up.

Training Tips   Get as much of the body behind the ball as possible. Make sure the upper body stays over the ball and the palms trap the ball against the body.

Variations

1. Vary the service. Some balls should be played with considerable velocity, others more accurately. Some serves should be ground balls, others directly to the waist area.
2. Play for time. Goalkeepers count how many balls they receive within one to two minutes.
3. Play competitively for a score. Any dropped ball counts as a point for the opponent. Any serve played beyond the keeper's reach counts against the serving goalkeeper.
4. Play for a specific time, three to five minutes, keeping score.

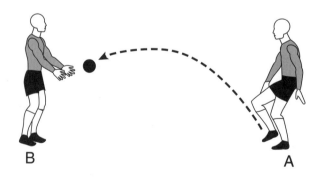

B   A

TURN AND SAVE

Individual Exercise

Equipment   2 balls

Organization   Three goalkeepers, A, B, and C, 8 to 10 yards apart in a straight line.

Procedure   Goalkeeper A plays the ball on the ground to Goalkeeper B, who scoops up the ball and returns it to Goalkeeper A. Keeper B then turns and receives another ball from Goalkeeper C and quickly returns it. Repeat 10 times and switch. Serves are either directly right at the keeper or a step or two to the side.

Training Tips   Keep feet alive and body bouncing.

Variations
1. Vary the service. Some balls should be played with considerable velocity, others more accurately. Some serves should be ground balls, others directly to the waist area.
2. Play for time. Goalkeepers play for a specific time, 30 to 90 seconds. Serves should occur without hesitation.
3. Play competitively for a score. Any ball not handled cleanly (directly into the chest) counts as a point for the opponent. Any serve played beyond the keeper's reach counts against the serving goalkeeper.
4. Play for a specific time, two to three minutes, keeping score.

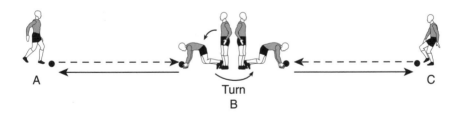

SCOOP AND SPRINT

Individual Exercise

Equipment   1 ball

Organization   Two pairs of goalkeepers are 8 to 10 yards apart.

Procedure   Goalkeepers A and B face two teammates (C and D). Keeper A serves a ground ball to C and then sprints to C's position. C scoops up the ball and plays the same type of serve to B, sprinting to B's position. B continues the exercise to D.

Training Tips   Goalkeepers should come forward to meet the ball, not wait for it.

Variation   Serve waist-high balls.

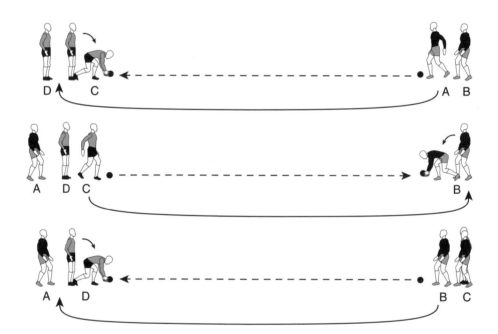

SAVING THE TWEENER BALL

Individual Exercise

Equipment   1 to 2 balls, 4 disks or cones

Organization   Two goalkeepers (A and B) face one another at a distance of 8 to 10 yards. Markers are placed 8 yards apart, with each goalkeeper's starting position on the cone.

Procedure   Goalkeeper A starts the exercise, rolling the ball toward the opposite marker of Goalkeeper B. The serve must be paced so that B does not wait for the serve with a standing save and does not have to dive. The serve should be paced so B uses the tweener save. When B receives A's serve, he or she then serves to A's opposite cone. Continue until each keeper has received 10 to 15 balls.

Training Tips   The goalkeeper receiving the serve uses proper footwork, shuffle or sprint, to get across the goal. The trailing leg should then drag behind, with the lead leg supporting the keeper's body weight. The upper trunk should twist and face the server to get as much body behind the ball as possible.

Variations

1. Use three goalkeepers and two balls. The exercise should be in the goal, or use two markers. Keepers A and B face each goalpost, 8 to 10 yards away and serve to C's opposite post.
2. Rotate after 10 to 15 receptions or play for 30- to 90-second intervals.

FORWARD VAULTS

Individual Exercise

Equipment   1 ball

Organization   Goalkeepers A and B kneel facing one another at a distance of five yards.

Procedure   Goalkeeper A bounces the ball to Goalkeeper B, who vaults forward to meet the ball. Keeper B returns to A in a similar manner. The exercise continues until each keeper has fielded 10 to 15 serves.

Training Tips   Receive the ball with palms up and forearms underneath the ball. Vault forward to meet the ball.

Variations

1. Use the same setup as above, but keepers start from a squatting position.
2. Goalkeepers now stand in a ready position and at a distance of about 10 yards apart. Keeper A throws a low hard serve toward B's feet. B vaults forward to make the save and then serves a similar ball to A. The keepers vary the trajectory and velocity of the serves.
3. The receiving goalkeeper stands one to two yards behind two markers three to four yards apart. Keeper A serves to Keeper B, who must vault forward and receive the ball before it crosses the line between the two markers.

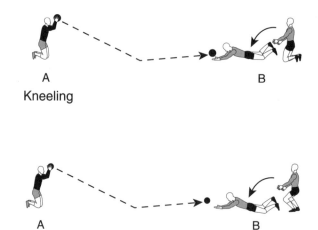

A
Kneeling

B

A
Squatting

B

SMOTHERING LOOSE BALLS

Individual Exercise

Equipment   1 ball

Organization   Goalkeeper stands holding a ball with feet spread shoulder-width apart.

Procedure   Keeper bends forward and rolls the ball through his or her legs, quickly turns, and then vaults backward to smother the ball by pinning it to the ground. Repeat at maximum speed for 30 seconds.

Training Tips   Always vault directly to the ball. Do not twist or turn. Arms should be completely outstretched with palms out to the side. The ball should immediately be pulled into the chest.

Variations

1. Goalkeepers A and B serve low, hard balls directly at each other from a kneeling position at a distance of five yards. The receiving keeper intentionally mishandles the ball, purposely batting the ball in front of his or her position and then vaults out to smother it.
2. Same as variation 1 but from a squatting position.
3. Goalkeepers now stand in a ready position at a distance of about 10 yards apart. Keeper A throws a low hard serve toward B's feet. B intentionally misplays the ball and then vaults forward to smother the ball. B then serves a similar ball to A. The keepers vary the trajectory and velocity of the serves. Serving keepers should also charge forward toward the receiving keeper to make the smothering technique realistic.

COLLECTING THROUGH BALLS

Individual Exercise

Equipment   1 ball

Organization   Goalkeepers A, B, and C form a straight line 10 to 15 yards apart. B stands with legs spread, midway between A and C.

Procedure   Goalkeeper A rolls the ball through B's legs toward C. C quickly moves forward and uses the forward vault technique to collect the ball. Keeper C vaults to the side of B after making the save. Players return to their original positions, then C rolls through B's legs, and A uses the forward vault to save. Continue for 30 to 40 seconds. Players then rotate positions.

Training Tips   Keepers need to vault forward and to the side to avoid the onrushing attacker, squeezing the ball to their chest on the scoop and landing on their forearms.

Variations   Goalkeepers A, B, and C become a server, a chaser, and a goalkeeper. Keeper A, the server with four to six balls, stands facing the goal at a distance of 25 to 30 yards. Keeper B is the chaser who stands beside A. Goalkeeper C is in the goal. The server pushes a slowly paced ball toward the penalty area; the chaser waits one second and then sprints to catch up to the ball. Goalkeeper C sprints forward off the goal line and then vaults forward, scoops the ball, and goes to the side of the onrushing chaser. Switch positions after several repetitions. Note that the chaser should let the goalkeeper win the race to the ball.

LOW BALL KEEPER WARS

Individual Exercise

Equipment   2 regulation portable goals, 4 markers (cones, disks, poles), 5 balls

Organization   Goals are about 12 to 20 yards apart, depending on the skill level of the keepers. One goalkeeper is in each goal. Mark a small goal by placing two markers in the center of the goal about two to four yards apart, again depending on the players' skill level.

Procedure   Goalkeeper A may throw, kick, or volley the ball between the markers of Goalkeeper B's goal. After the shot is taken by A, B then shoots on A. Keepers can take only one step before throwing or kicking. Shots must be below head height. Keepers cannot dive to save. Play for a time limit and keep score. Scores count only when they are between the markers and below head height.

Training Tips   Goalkeepers should be using only the techniques of a standing save for a ground ball or waist-high ball, a tweener save, or a forward vault.

Variations

1. Award two points for a goal (between the markers), but award one point to the receiving keeper for any shot placed outside the markers or above head height.
2. Make any rebounds live balls and let the shooting keeper attempt to score.

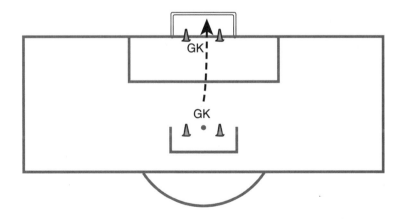

LOW AND MEDIUM BALL REPETITIONS

Group Exercise

Equipment   2 to 3 balls

Organization   Two goalkeepers, two balls, and 8 to 10 field players are spread out in an area about the size of the penalty area, 18 × 44 yards.

Procedure   Players interpass and, on goalkeeper's command, play a ground ball directly to the keeper. Goalkeeper then distributes to the nearest open player and demands a different ball. Play is continuous for 5 to 10 minutes.

Training Tips   Goalkeepers should be assertive and demand the ball, using correct technique, especially when moving forward to meet the ball.

Variations

1. Players strike a waist-high ball to the goalkeeper.
2. Keeper distributes to a field player, who immediately plays it back to the goalkeeper.
3. Keeper distributes to a field player, who immediately plays it to another player; that player passes the ball back to the goalkeeper.
4. Players distribute with instep and outside of the foot as well as the inside of the foot to replicate different services.

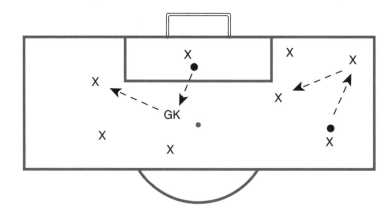

TWEENER REPETITIONS

Group Exercise

Equipment   2 to 3 balls

Organization   Two goalkeepers, two balls, and 8 to 10 field players are spread out in an area about the size of the penalty area, 18 × 44 yards.

Procedure   Players interpass and, on goalkeeper's command, play a ground ball just to the left or right of the keeper. Keeper shuffles several yards to the side and kneels, using a tweener technique to scoop up the ball. Goalkeeper then distributes to the nearest open player and demands a different ball. Play continues for 5 to 10 minutes.

Training Tips   Goalkeepers should be assertive and demand the ball, using correct tweener technique, especially when moving forward to meet the ball.

Variations

1. Keeper distributes to a field player, who immediately plays it back to the goalkeeper.
2. Keeper distributes to a field player, who immediately plays it to another player, and that player passes the ball first time back to the keeper.

THREE LINES OF SHOOTERS

Group Exercise

Equipment   16 balls, 1 regulation goal, markers

Organization   Three lines of shooters line up about 12 to 18 yards from the goal. A cone or disk marks each starting position of the shooters. One line should be central to the goal; the other two lines should be at an angle to the left and right of center. Small goals about three to four yards should be marked in the goal facing the shooting line. One keeper is between the marked goal, facing the shooter.

Procedure   Shooter A, on the left side, hits a shot to the marked goal directly in front of him or her. The keeper saves using a standing scoop save. Shooter B, on the center line, shoots, and then Shooter C shoots on the opposite side. Repeat the procedure with the next line of shooters, all trying to beat the keeper with a shot directly at him or her. The same keeper should field 9 to 12 shots or 3 to 4 times through the circuit.

Training Tips   Shots should be low and hard and directly at the keeper. Goalkeepers should try to save using a standing scoop save, a tweener save, or a forward vault. The keeper is not allowed to dive in this exercise. The purpose is for the feet to move using a quick side shuffle to get as much of the body as possible behind the ball. Shooters should wait until the keeper is set before shooting.

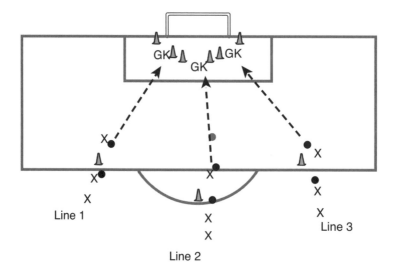

Line 1

Line 2

Line 3

Variations

1. Gradually pick up the pace of the exercise so that the goalkeeper must hustle to get to the next goal.
2. The goalkeeper's starting position must be behind the markers so that he or she has to use the forward vault to receive the ball before it crosses the imaginary line between the cones or markers.
3. Any mishandled ball is live, so the keeper must smother the ball under pressure.

SMALL-SIDED GAME

Team Exercise

Equipment   2 regulation portable goals, 16 balls, markers

Organization   Play 4 v 4 in a field about 20 × 35 yards. Place two markers in the center of the goal about three to four yards apart.

Procedure   The goalkeeper defends the central marked goal, and players shoot between the markers. Any mishandled ball is live, so the keeper must smother the ball under pressure.

Training Tips   Because the goal is so narrow, the great majority of saves should be standing saves, tweener saves, forward vaults, or smothers.

Variations

1. Place the markers two yards from the goal line, but make the goalkeeper stand on the goal line. The goalkeeper is not allowed in front of or between the marked goal until the shot is taken, forcing the keeper to use the forward vault to save.

2. Give two points for a goal but one point to the team whose goalkeeper makes a save without diving.

3. Divide the field in thirds and do not allow the attacking team in the final third to ensure more long-range shooting, which requires more standing saves.

4. Construct two goals three yards wide and one yard apart from each other. The goalkeeper has to cover both goals, ensuring quick foot movement as he or she goes back and forth between the two goals.

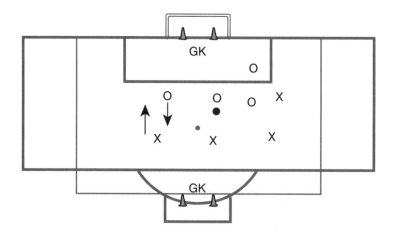

Controlling High Balls and Crosses

In soccer, a high ball is defined as any ball arriving at the goalkeeper's chest or above. Crosses are driven balls swerved into the goalmouth from a flank area of the field. Receiving and controlling high balls and crosses presents a unique and difficult challenge for the goalkeeper. In many instances, the ball must be fielded while fending off the physical challenge of a goal-hungry opponent attempting to head the ball into the goal. At other times, the keeper may have to go up in a crowd of players, teammates as well as opponents, to secure the ball. As a consequence, several methods are used to receive high balls and crosses.

The choice of technique is based on factors such as the height, velocity, and flight path of the ball. For example, a ball arriving at chest level is received in a different manner than a ball arriving above the keeper's head. The keeper's approach to the ball, as well as the position of the hands and body as the ball arrives, also depends on the nature of the service. A ball crossed into the goal area is received in a slightly different manner from a ball coming directly at the goal. Environmental factors such as rain, wind, and snow must also be taken into account, as poor weather conditions make it much more difficult for the keeper to catch and hold the ball. In all cases, the position of the keeper's head and hands as the ball arrives is of critical importance.

Position of the Hands: The W Catch

A ball arriving at chest height or above is received with the hands held in what is commonly referred to as the "W," or window, position. Fingers are spread and extended toward the oncoming ball with thumbs almost, but not quite, touching behind. Forearms are positioned behind the ball, parallel to one another (figure 4.1). The ball is received on the fingertips while the hands simultaneously withdraw to cushion the impact.

KEY ELEMENTS OF PEAK PERFORMANCE

The W Catch

1. Spread fingers and extend them toward the ball.
2. Position thumbs behind the ball with palms to side.
3. Position forearms parallel to one another.
4. Receive the ball on the fingertips.
5. Withdraw hands as the ball arrives to cushion the impact.
6. Develop "soft and silent hands." There should be little or no sound as the ball contacts the hands.

Figure 4.1 The W catch.

Position of the Head: HEH Principle

The Hands-Eyes-Head (HEH) Principle describes the proper alignment of hands and head as the ball arrives. To execute HEH properly, the keeper positions in a direct line with the oncoming ball with shoulders square, extending arms toward the ball with hands positioned in the "W." The head is positioned directly behind the hands as if looking through the window formed by the thumbs and index fingers. Keep the head steady with vision focused on the ball (figure 4.2). The ball is received with the hands in the "W" position and then secured against the chest. Make sure thumbs are nearly touching behind the ball as it arrives, so that the ball does not slip between the hands. This is particularly important if the playing conditions are wet and the ball slippery.

KEY ELEMENTS OF PEAK PERFORMANCE

The HEH Principle

1. Position body in direct line with the oncoming ball.
2. Face the ball with shoulders square.
3. Position hands and head in direct line with the oncoming ball.

Figure 4.2 The HEH technique.

4. Look through the window formed by the thumbs and index fingers.

5. "Watch" the ball directly into the hands.

Chest-High and Head-High Balls

A ball arriving at chest or head height is received using the same basic technique. The keeper faces the ball with shoulders square and hands positioned at chest height and palms facing forward. Feet plant approximately shoulder-width apart. Arms extend to meet the ball as it arrives, with forearms parallel and with slight flexion at the elbows. Hands position in a W with fingers spread and thumbs almost touching behind. The keeper can look through the window formed by the thumbs and index fingers to follow the flight of the ball directly into his or her hands. In contrast to the technique used to receive a rolling or medium-height ball where the ball was allowed to roll up and onto the forearms, the keeper attempts to catch the chest- and head-high ball. Fingertips and palms position behind the upper half of the ball (figure 4.3). With hands positioned behind the upper half of the ball, it's less likely that the ball will skim off the fingers into the goal. Arms withdraw as the ball arrives to cushion the impact, and it is immediately secured to the chest. In the event of a physical challenge from an opponent, a solid base of support is maintained when receiving the ball.

> ### KEY ELEMENTS OF PEAK PERFORMANCE
>
> ### Receiving Chest- and Head-High Balls
>
> 1. Align body with oncoming ball.
> 2. Square shoulders with feet approximately shoulder-width apart.
> 3. Extend arms toward the ball with hands positioned in a W.
> 4. Align hands, eyes, and head with the ball.
> 5. Receive the ball on fingertips with palms positioned behind and to the side of the ball.
> 6. Withdraw arms on contact with the ball to cushion impact.
> 7. Secure the ball to the chest.

The Catchable High Ball

Controlling the area front and center of the goal is of paramount importance for the goalkeeper, as the majority of the opponent's scoring op-

Figure 4.3 Catching a head-high ball, with forearms parallel.

portunities originate there. With that in mind, the keeper must be able to deal with high balls and crosses driven into the goalmouth. As a rule, the goalkeeper should attempt to catch the high ball rather than box or parry it out of danger (see The Uncatchable High Ball later in this chapter). Success in receiving and holding the high ball depends on a combination of factors—proper receiving technique, optimal balance and body control, sound judgment, and supreme confidence in the ability to get the job done.

In preparing to receive the high ball, the keeper faces the ball with shoulders square and takes a moment to judge the trajectory before moving toward the ball in preparation to leave the ground. The jumping technique looks similar to that of a layup in basketball. In most cases, the goalkeeper uses a one-leg takeoff to generate maximum upward momentum. Arms and hands extend upward in one fluid motion to catch the ball at the highest possible point. It's important to jump off the correct foot. To receive a ball crossed from the flank, thrust the outside leg (leg nearest to the field) upward with the knee flexed and pointed toward the ball. In this position, the goalkeeper is protected from an onrushing opponent also attempting to jump and head the ball. The keeper's inside leg (leg nearest the goal) remains straight to provide balance and to serve as a stabilizing point upon return to the ground (figure 4.4). The arms and outside leg thrust upward, with hands positioned in the W. The ball is received at the highest point possible and then brought down and secured against the chest.

The goalkeeper makes two critical decisions when receiving a ball crossed from the flank: (1) when to initiate movement toward the ball, and (2) when to leave the ground and go airborne. The keeper doesn't want to commit too early. To arrive at the best possible decision, he or she must swiftly analyze the situation and determine answers to the following questions. What is the trajectory of the ball—is it rising or beginning to descend? Is it driven with force or softly lofted into the goal area? Is the ball swerving away from the goal (out-swinger) or bending inward (in-swinger)? Are opponents positioned nearby who will challenge for the ball?

Once the decision to move forward has been made, the move must be executed with speed and confidence. Coaches often refer to this as the "come late, come hard" rule. The keeper should take the most direct route to the spot where he or she will go airborne to intercept the flight path of the ball. Proper timing of the approach is critical. The keeper should be moving forward (toward the ball) at the moment he or she leaves the ground. The ball should be received at the highest possible point.

KEY ELEMENTS OF PEAK PERFORMANCE

Receiving the Catchable High Ball

1. Face the ball with shoulders square.
2. Move toward the ball in preparation to initiate the jump.
3. Keep head steady with vision focused on the ball.
4. Use a one-leg takeoff to leave the ground.
5. Thrust arms and outside leg (nearest to the field) upward in one fluid motion.
6. Keep the inside (balance) leg straight.
7. Position hands in the W.
8. Employ the HEH principle.
9. Receive the ball on fingertips at the highest point of the jump.
10. Withdraw arms and secure the ball to the chest.

Figure 4.4 Catching the high ball.

High-Ball Drills

The ability of the goalkeeper to handle high balls and crosses might be the single most important element of goalkeeping. Thus, this area merits serious attention and should be addressed in virtually every training session. The following exercises are designed to improve the goalkeeper's ability to deal with many types of serves. As with any drill, the quality of the serve is crucial to the success of the exercise. The individual exercises are fundamental and designed to improve individual techniques. The goalkeeper needs to be well schooled in the fundamentals before compounding the situation with split-second decision making. The group and team drills provided here include more gamelike situations. These exercises require the keeper to make important decisions, such as when to release to the ball and whether to catch it or box it away from the goalmouth.

STEP AND CATCH

Individual Exercise

Equipment   1 ball

Organization   Two goalkeepers, A and B, face each other, three to five yards apart.

Procedure   Goalkeeper A tosses the ball to the right or left of Goalkeeper B, who takes a step sideways to the ball and receives it. Goalkeeper B repeats to Goalkeeper A.

Training Tips   Keeper receiving the ball uses W catch technique and receives the ball using HEH.

Variations

1. Vary the service. Some balls should be played with considerable velocity, others more accurately. Gradually pick up the pace of the serves.
2. Play for time. Goalkeepers must count how many balls they receive within one to two minutes.
3. Play competitively for a score. Any dropped ball counts as a point for the opponent. Any serve played beyond the keeper's reach counts against the serving goalkeeper.
4. Play for a specific time, three to five minutes, and keep score.

CATCHING CHEST- AND HEAD-HIGH BALLS

Individual Exercise

Equipment   2 balls

Organization   Goalkeepers A, B, and C position in a straight line. Goal-keepers A and C, each with a ball, face one another at a distance of 10 yards, with B between them.

Procedure   Keeper A tosses a chest-high or head-high ball to B, who receives with a W catch but with palms on top rather than behind the ball. Keeper B returns the ball to A and quickly turns to receive a ball tossed by C. Continue for 60 seconds and then rotate players.

Training Tips   Forearms should be parallel to each other, with elbows tucked in.

Variation   Same setup, but servers volley the ball out of the hands. Vary pace of serve.

A   B   C

CATCHING BALLS ABOVE THE HEAD

Individual Exercise

Equipment   1 ball

Organization   Keeper stands holding the ball.

Procedure   The keeper works on a one-leg takeoff by jumping into the air with the ball.

Training Tips   Arms and leg thrust into the air simultaneously, arms completely stretched above the head.

Variations
1. Alternate leg for takeoff.
2. Toss ball into the air, use one-leg takeoff to catch the ball at the highest point. Continue to alternate leg for takeoff.

CATCHING HIGH BALLS GOING SIDE TO SIDE

Individual Exercise

Equipment   1 ball, 3 flags or cones

Organization   Three flags are organized in a triangle, approximately eight yards apart. The goalkeeper starts at the apex of the triangle. The coach or server stands about five yards in front of the base of the triangle, or the goal.

Procedure   The coach tosses or volleys a high ball toward one of the flags. The keeper must go forward and catch the ball at the highest point using the proper takeoff leg. For example, if the serve is to the keeper's left, the left leg is used. After catching the ball, the keeper returns it to the server and uses proper footwork to return to the starting point. Continue for 60 seconds.

Training Tips   The goalkeeper thrusts the leg into the air for momentum and shoulders should square up to the server.

Variations

1. The goalkeeper receives a ground ball, returns it to the server, and then runs forward to catch the high ball.
2. The goalkeeper must come forward to catch a high ball in front and in the middle of the flags, quickly return to the starting point, and go either left or right to catch the next serve.
3. The keeper must do a forward roll, jump up or perform some other action, and then go forward.

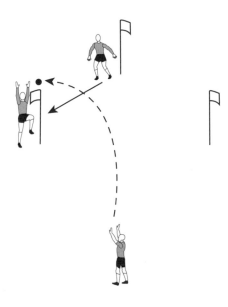

HIGH-BALL REPETITIONS

Group Exercise

Equipment   6 balls, 1 goal

Organization   Two goalkeepers, 6 balls, and 8 to 10 field players spread out in an area approximately one-half the field.

Procedure   Players interpass and, on coach's command, play a chipped ball directly to the keeper. Goalkeeper then distributes to the nearest open player and demands a different ball. Play goes continuously for 5 to 10 minutes.

Training Tips   Goalkeepers should be assertive and demand the ball, using correct technique to receive it. Keepers catch the ball above the head or use the W catch. Players serving the ball should vary the type of service (driven ball, lofted ball, out-swinger, in-swinger, etc.).

Variations
1. Players strike a waist-high ball to the goalkeeper.
2. Keeper distributes to a field player in the air who immediately volleys it back to the goalkeeper.
3. Keeper distributes a high ball to a field player who must head the ball to the goalkeeper.
4. Keeper distributes to a field player who immediately plays it to another player, and that player chips the ball back to the keeper.

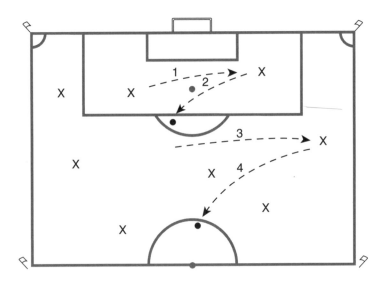

CATCHING CROSSES

Group Exercise

Equipment   6 balls, 2 portable goals

Organization   Place the portable goals facing each other about 25 yards apart but at opposite ends of the penalty area. Players should position next to the goal in the space between the edge of the penalty area and the touchline.

Procedure   Goalkeeper A rolls the ball ahead to the first player on his or her side, who serves a cross into Goalkeeper B, who catches the cross and then quickly distributes to a player on that side, who repeats the exercise.

There should be three to four players to the side of each goal. Once a player has taken a cross, he or she moves behind the line of players of the opposite goal.

Training Tips   The goalkeeper focuses on technique and decision-making. The decision-making is whether to catch the cross or leave it and call "away." Servers should vary the type of service.

Variations

1. After the player takes a cross, he or she then takes a position in front of the goal to attack the next cross.
2. Add a permanent defender so that there's a 1 v 1 situation in front of the goal and the goalkeeper must communicate with the defender.
3. Instead of waiting in line, a second player joins in in front of the goal, so now there's a 2 v 1 situation, increasing the goalkeeper's decisions. One attacker should make a near post run, another a far post run.

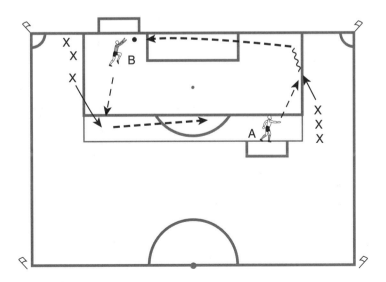

HIGH-BALL PRESSURE TRAINING

Group Exercise

Equipment   16 balls, 2 goals (1 portable)

Organization   The field is the penalty area (18 × 44 yards); place the portable goal at the edge of the penalty area, facing the other goal. Organize players into two teams: 3 v 3 or 4 v 4. Have two to four servers position in the flank area outside the penalty area.

Procedure   Servers cross balls into the goal area. The goalkeeper must aggressively go and catch the ball and then distribute to the opposite flank, where another cross is taken. Both teams can attack either goal—in other words, there are no defenders. Any cross is a live ball if the goalkeeper cannot catch it. Any team can score but only on the goalkeeper for which the cross was originally intended. Teams should keep score.

Training Tips   Goalkeepers must be aggressive but still need to decide which crosses they can go for and which are out of their range. This exercise is intended to force keepers to extend their range.

Variations

1. Have each team defend a goal so that there's communication between the keeper and the defenders and increased decision making.
2. Allow the server the option of dribbling into the penalty area to change the angle of the cross and create a numbers-up situation for the team trying to score. This forces the goalkeeper to adjust positioning.
3. Allow goalkeepers to box or catch the ball.

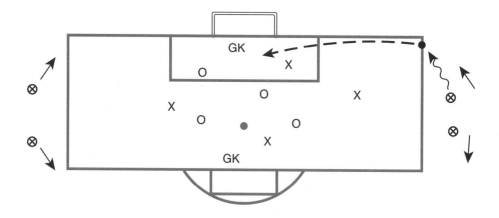

3 v 2 CROSSING GAME

Group Exercise

Equipment   16 balls, 2 goals (1 portable)

Organization   Set up the portable goal at midfield to play in half the field. Divide this area into two halves, using markers to separate each half. Place markers a few yards in from the touchline to create channels for unopposed flank players. Use two flank players in each channel. There should be a 3 v 2 situation in each area in front of the goals: three attackers and two defenders.

Procedure   Goalkeeper A throws a ball to a flank player. Keepers can use any flank player; they are not restricted to distribute to a certain player. The flank player should then serve a quality cross into the area. If Goalkeeper B catches the cross, he or she then throws the ball out to another flank player, and the play develops toward the opposite goal. Any cross not caught but dropping into the playing area is a live ball, resulting in a 3 v 2 situation to goal.

Training Tips   Keepers should be encouraged to distribute to the opposite flank from where the cross originated. Goalkeepers need to adjust their positioning to the origin of the serve as well as the positioning of the field players. Field players need to make precise runs. Communication and decision making are key components for this exercise.

Variations
1. Flank players may pass to each other before crossing.
2. Flank players may dribble from their channel, where they are unopposed, to create a live 4 v 2 situation. This forces an adjustment in the positioning of the goalkeeper.
3. A defender may join the attack.

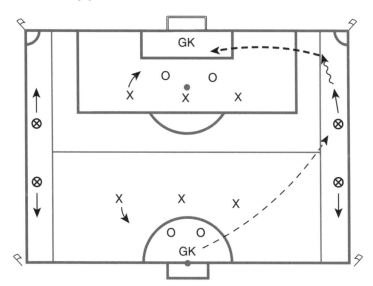

6 v 6 + 2 CROSSING GAME

Team Exercise

Equipment   10 balls, marking disks, 2 goals (1 portable)

Organization   Set up the portable goal about 18 yards beyond the half-way line and create a penalty area with markers. Divide the field into thirds. Create a channel a few yards in from the touchline. Organize two teams of six field players and provide each team with two flank players, one in each channel. Have balls supplied in both goals and with a coach at midfield.

Procedure   A coach starts the play at midfield. The object is for the possessing team to play a ball into the attack third for their flank player, who should then prepare the ball for a cross. After any change of possession, players are restricted to play to one of the flank players before the goal can be attacked. Field players also cannot go into the attack third until the ball is played into that area. Once the ball enters the attack third, all players, attacking and defending, can enter to win the cross. The keeper restarts with a goal kick any ball that goes over the endline. The coach at midfield restarts any ball over the touchline. This ensures a free-flowing activity and manipulates the conditions of the exercise.

Training Tips   In addition to the technical skills of catching crosses, goalkeepers should be involved with the tactical decisions of organization, communication, distribution, and support in the attack. This exercise should focus on goalkeeper organization and communication of his or her defenders, especially as they recover into their defending third.

Variations

1. Remove the restriction that after a change of possession the ball must be played to the flank players. Allow the game to dictate this.
2. Allow flank players to dribble from their channel, where they are unopposed, to create a live numbers-up (7 v 6) situation. This forces the keeper to adjust positioning.
3. Remove channels completely and play 8 v 8, still emphasizing crosses.
4. Remove field markers dividing the thirds of the field and use coaches or extra players to call offside. Emphasize to the defending team to step up away from the goal.

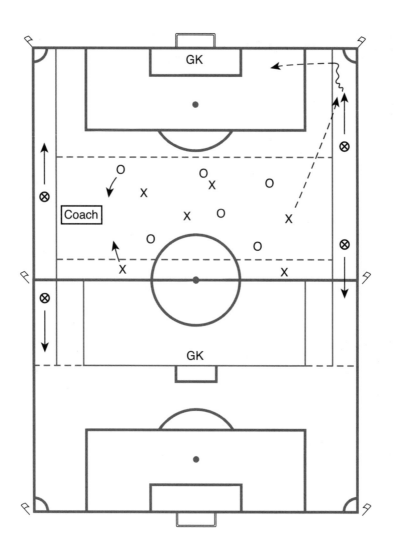

The Uncatchable High Ball

In most cases the keeper can catch and secure a high ball served into the goal area. However, some situations dictate otherwise. For example, the keeper might have difficulty judging the flight of a ball that is dipping or swerving as it enters the goal area. Wet and windy playing conditions can create doubt about whether a ball can be caught cleanly. Opposing forwards may aggressively challenge for the ball as the keeper attempts to receive it. Whatever the case, if the goalkeeper is unsure of holding the ball, it's prudent to choose safety first rather than risk a costly error. Rather than attempting to catch the ball, the keeper should box, or punch, it away from the danger area front and center of the goal.

The decision whether to catch or box the high ball is a critical one. Poor decisions lead to errors that might determine the outcome of the game. In general, the keeper should attempt to box rather than catch the ball if one or more of the following conditions are present:

- The goal mouth is crowded with players and the path to the ball partially blocked.
- There is strong likelihood of a collision with an opponent challenging for the ball.
- The goalkeeper is knocked off balance when jumping upward to receive the ball.
- The ball is slippery due to rain, snow, or sleet.
- Footing is poor and the keeper is unsure if he or she can get to the ball.
- Other factors raise doubts in the keeper's mind about his or her ability to safely secure the ball.

A keeper can box the uncatchable high ball with one or both hands. The choice of technique depends on the trajectory of the ball as it approaches the goal, the goalkeeper's position in relation to the ball and opponents, and the keeper's confidence level in his or her ability to perform the boxing technique.

Two-Fisted Boxing

The two-fisted boxing technique is most often used in situations where the keeper can move directly toward the oncoming ball with shoulders square to the ball. The primary objective is to direct the ball away from the goalmouth into a less dangerous scoring area. This is accomplished by boxing the ball high, far, and wide toward a flank area of the field. Boxing the ball high into the air gives defending players precious moments to regroup and organize. Boxing the ball as far as possible, ideally outside of the penalty area, reduces the risk of an opponent immediately sending a shot back at goal as the ball drops to the ground. Boxing the ball toward the flank area removes the ball from the dangerous scoring zone immediately front and center of the goal, an area where an opportunistic opponent has the advantage of a wide shooting angle to goal.

To execute the two-fisted technique, the keeper forms two solid fists with knuckles facing forward and thumbs on top. Hands position side by side, with wrists firm. Arms remain tightly against the sides, with elbows flexed about 90 degrees. As the ball arrives, arms and fists extend in unison to meet it (figure 4.5a). A short, compact, explosive-type movement is used rather than a looping movement. Wrists remain firm and fists stay together as they contact the ball just below its horizontal midline. The keeper attempts to box the ball at the highest possible point (figure 4.5b).

Figure 4.5 Two-fisted boxing: *(a)* as the ball arrives and *(b)* follow-through.

Two-Fisted Boxing

1. Square shoulders and hips toward the oncoming ball.
2. Move toward the ball in preparation to box the ball.
3. Position fists side by side with wrists firm.
4. Keep elbows flexed and tight to sides.
5. Use a short powerful extension of arms.
6. Contact the ball at highest possible point.
7. Box the ball high, far, and wide of the goal area.

One-Fisted Boxing

A ball driven from the flank and traveling across the goalmouth poses a different challenge for the goalkeeper. Because the ball is moving at a high velocity and is not coming directly at the goal, the keeper should continue the ball's flight toward the opposite flank rather than try to box it back in the direction from where it came. To do so, the keeper boxes across the body, using a one-fisted boxing technique. For example, a ball crossed from the opponent's left flank (goalkeeper's right) is boxed with the right hand so as to continue its flight toward the keeper's left flank. A ball served across the goal area from the opponent's right flank (keeper's left) is boxed with the left hand toward the keeper's right flank. The boxing motion should be compact and powerful. A short, explosive extension of the arm angled across the body provides the greatest degree of control. The fist remains tight and the wrist firm.

The one-fisted boxing technique is also appropriate for rare occasions when the goalkeeper is caught off the goal line with a high ball dropping behind him or her. If the keeper does not have sufficient time to backpedal and catch the ball, he or she can use the one-fisted boxing technique to punch the ball over the crossbar and out of play. To do so, the keeper takes a deep dropstep with the foot farthest from the ball, angles the body sideways, and boxes the ball over the bar with a short, powerful extension of the opposite arm (figure 4.6).

Keepers should follow these two simple rules when boxing a ball dropping behind them near the crossbar: (1) to box a ball dropping over the left shoulder, take a dropstep left and box across the body with the right hand; (2) to box a ball dropping over the right shoulder, take a dropstep right and box across the body with the left hand.

Figure 4.6 One-fisted boxing: *(a)* initial contact and *(b)* follow-through.

KEY ELEMENTS OF PEAK PERFORMANCE

One-Fisted Boxing

1. Use the one-fisted technique to box a high ball crossed into the goalmouth or a ball dropping behind you.

2. When boxing a crossed ball, continue its flight toward the opposite touchline.

3. When boxing a ball dropping behind you, take a dropstep and bring the opposite arm across the chest.

4. Use a short, powerful extension of the arm and fist.

5. Focus vision on the ball throughout the boxing motion.

Open-Palm Technique

The open-palm is another method of handling a high ball dropping behind the keeper. This technique is actually preferable to boxing the ball because it provides a greater degree of control. Rather than using a closed fist to propel the ball over the bar, the keeper simply guides the ball over the goal with the open hand. This is commonly called "turning" or "palming" the ball over the bar. One or two hands can be used to palm the ball. In most situations, the one-hand technique is preferable. The mechanics are similar to those used when boxing with one fist. The technique begins with a dropstep with the foot farthest from the ball. For example, the keeper dropsteps with the left foot when preparing to handle a ball crossed from his or her right (opponent's left) side that is dropping over his or her left shoulder. At the proper moment, the keeper projects the right arm and hand upward and across the body to palm the ball over the goal (figure 4.7). He or she uses the opposite (nonpalming) hand to "feel" for the crossbar. Touching the bar gives a better idea of position in relation to the goal. After turning the ball over the bar, the keeper rotates to face the ground as he or she falls. Arms and hands contact the ground first. The keeper tucks and rolls to further cushion the impact.

A powerfully driven shot arriving directly above the goalkeeper's head can be deflected over the crossbar using a two-hand palming technique. This skill is most appropriate for young keepers who lack the strength and vertical leap to successfully execute the one-hand palming technique. To palm the ball, a keeper positions hands side by side with palms facing forward and angled back slightly from vertical. The ball is contacted just below its horizontal midline, with wrists held firm. As the ball arrives, arms extend and hands move upward to alter the flight path upward and over the crossbar.

KEY ELEMENTS OF PEAK PERFORMANCE

Open-Palm Technique

1. Use the one-hand technique to turn a ball dropping over the right shoulder. Dropstep with the right foot and palm the ball with the left hand.
2. Use the one-hand technique to turn a ball dropping over the left shoulder. Dropstep with the left foot and turn the ball with the right hand.
3. Use the two-hand palming technique to deflect a powerfully driven ball traveling directly at or above the head.
4. Position palms forward with hands angled slightly back.
5. Contact the lower half of the ball with wrists firm.
6. Deflect the ball upward and over the crossbar.
7. Keep the head steady and vision focused on the ball at all times.

Uncatchable High-Ball Drills

Ideally, we would like the keeper to catch and secure every ball, but that's just not possible in some situations. Thus, every keeper needs to perfect

Figure 4.7 Palming the ball over the goal: (a) as the ball approaches and (b) follow-through.

the techniques used to handle shots or crosses that are uncatchable. Exercises that follow are designed to improve the goalkeeper's ability to execute various techniques used to deal with uncatchable high balls. The quality of the serve is crucial to the success of these drills. *The serves must be accurate.* If the servers are having difficulty striking accurate balls, have them volley the ball out of their hands. Thrown balls should be used only as a last resort, as it's preferable for the keeper to see the rotation of the ball from the foot.

The individual exercises that follow are fundamental in nature and designed to improve the keeper's ability to perform the individual techniques of one- or two-fisted boxing, as well as palming the ball. The group and team exercises incorporate more gamelike pressure. They force the goalkeeper not only to decide when and if he or she should go to the ball but what technique should be used.

FUNDAMENTAL TWO-FISTED BOXING

Individual Exercise

Equipment   2 to 4 balls

Organization   Three goalkeepers (A, B, C) form a straight line about five yards apart. Goalkeeper B is in the middle and is the server. Goalkeeper A faces B and C.

Procedure   Keeper B tosses a ball to Keeper A, who is sitting. Keeper A boxes the ball over Keeper B's head to Keeper C. Keeper A boxes the ball 10 times, then the keepers rotate positions.

Training Tips   The focus is purely on the thrust of the arms and the fists to achieve height and distance. Forearms need to be parallel, with the power coming from the chest.

Variations

1. Progress from a sitting position to kneeling, then squatting, and finally to a standing position. Once in a standing position, distance between servers and the keeper increases from 5 yards to 10 to 15 yards.
2. Once the keeper is comfortable with the simple technique of boxing, progress to using the pressure of a time limit—that is, have Keeper A box as many balls as possible in a 30- to 40-second time period.
3. Have Keeper A start in a push-up position and then spring to his or her feet to box the ball.

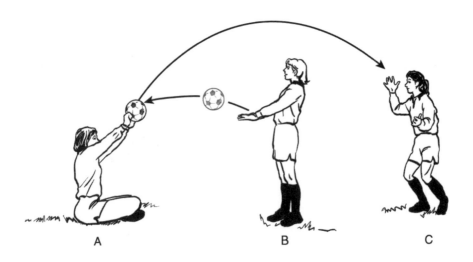

A   B   C

FUNDAMENTAL ONE-FISTED BOXING

Individual Exercise

Equipment   2 to 4 balls

Organization   Three goalkeepers (A, B, C) form a straight line about five yards apart. Goalkeeper B is in the middle and kneeling perpendicular between A and C. Goalkeepers A and C face each other.

Procedure   Keeper A tosses a ball above Keeper B's head. Keeper B continues the flight of the ball by fisting it across the body to Keeper C. Keeper C serves another toss to Keeper B, who continues the flight by boxing it with the opposite fist back to Keeper A. Keeper B boxes the ball 10 times; keepers then rotate positions.

Training Tips   *Serves must be accurate.* If Keeper B is to box with the right hand, then the toss should be over the left shoulder and vice versa. The keeper must concentrate on getting the fist underneath the bottom half of the ball and thrusting the fist in a short jabbing motion.

Variations

1. Progress from kneeling to squatting and finally to a standing position. Once in a standing position, the distance between servers and the keeper increases from 5 yards to 10 to 15 yards.

2. Once the keeper is comfortable with this technique, progress to using the pressure of a time limit—that is, have Keeper B box as many balls as possible in a 30- to 40-second time period.

3. Have Keeper B start in a push-up position and then spring to his or her feet to fist the ball.

BOXING OVER THE OPPONENT

Individual Exercise

Equipment   2 to 4 balls

Organization   There are two pairs of goalkeepers (A-B and C-D). Keepers A and B stand between C and D, who are 10 to 15 yards apart. Keepers C and D are the servers and each has a ball.

Procedure   Keeper C tosses a high ball to Keeper A, who must box the ball with two fists over Keeper B back to Keeper C. Keepers A and B then turn and face Keeper D, who also serves a high ball to Keeper B, who boxes over Keeper A back to Keeper D. Continue for 10 repetitions each and then switch positions.

Training Tips   *Serves must be accurate.* Serves should be high enough to allow the goalkeeper the opportunity to time the approach and jump over the opponent and box through the ball correctly.

Variations

1. Employ the one-fisted technique so the goalkeeper can continue the flight by boxing the ball to the opposite server.
2. Add pressure of time so keepers box as many balls as possible in a 60-second time limit.
3. The keeper not boxing gradually increases the level and intensity of the challenge. The challenging keeper jumps with the keeper and uses legal shoulder charges.
4. Try having no designated boxer. The two keepers in the middle battle for live balls.

D

A   A   B

C

FUNDAMENTAL PALMING (TURNING)

Individual Exercise

Equipment   2 to 4 balls

Organization   Three goalkeepers (A, B, and C) form a straight line five yards apart. Keepers A and C face each other, and Keeper B is in the middle facing Keeper A.

Procedure   Goalkeeper A tosses a high ball over Keeper B's right shoulder. Keeper B takes a dropstep with the right foot and palms the ball to Keeper C using the left hand. Keeper C then serves over Keeper B's left shoulder, who takes a left-foot dropstep and turns the ball to Keeper A, using the right hand. Keeper B takes five serves with each hand and then switches.

Training Tips   *Serves must be accurate.* Serves should be high enough to allow the goalkeeper a chance to take a dropstep and palm the ball across the body. The palm should be slightly cupped so that there's no "slapping" sound. The palm should be placed under the bottom half of the ball so that the ball is directed up, not down. The head remains steady, and eyes follow the ball into the hands of the next server.

Variations

1. Add pressure of time so that keepers palm as many balls as possible in 60 seconds.
2. Have the keeper take several steps toward the server and react to the toss.

TURNING OVER THE CROSSBAR

Individual Exercise

Equipment   6 to 10 balls, 1 regulation goal

Organization   There are three servers and one goalkeeper. Servers A and C position at the intersection of the goal area and the endline. Server B stations 10 yards out, facing the goal. Each server has two or three balls.

Procedure   Server A tosses a high ball above the crossbar. The goalkeeper turns the ball safely out of play with an open palm. The keeper then faces Server C, who tosses the same type of serve. The keeper turns this ball over with the other hand. The keeper then goes toward Server B, who tosses a high ball behind the keeper toward the crossbar. The keeper takes a dropstep and correctly turns the ball over the bar. Continue until the keeper has received two to four tosses from each server.

Training Tips   *Serves must be accurate.* Serves should be high enough to allow the keeper a chance to use correct technique. The keeper should never lose sight of the ball and always follow it safely out of play. Server B alternates placement of the serve (i.e., right shoulder, then left shoulder). Careful attention should be paid to correct footwork.

Variations
1. Add pressure of time so that keepers palm as many balls as possible in a 60-second time limit.
2. Add the pressure of a challenging opponent. The intensity of the challenge should increase from simply standing with the keeper to jumping with the keeper to legally charging the keeper.

FUNCTIONAL CROSSES

Group Exercise

Equipment   10 balls, 1 regulation goal

Organization   Four servers position outside the penalty area with a supply of balls. Servers A and B station on each flank, Servers C and D about 30 yards out, facing the goal. The keeper positions to defend the goal.

Procedure   Servers A and B serve from the flank, and then Servers C and D serve into the goal. The keeper must box or palm the ball to safety, depending on the flight of the ball. Do two to four repetitions for each server.

Training Tips   *Serves must be accurate.* Serves should be high enough to allow the keeper the opportunity to use correct technique. If servers have trouble striking accurate balls, have them volley the ball out of their hands—throw only as a last resort, as it's preferable for the keeper to see the rotation of the ball off the foot.

The flank servers attempt to place balls in front of the keeper to use a two-fisted clearance and also serve balls across the keeper so the one-fisted box is used to continue the flight to the opposite flank. Servers C and D serve balls in front of the keeper for the two-fisted box but also behind the keeper so he or she can turn the ball over the crossbar. Servers should vary velocity, trajectory, and rotation of the cross.

Variations

1. Add pressure of time so that keepers play as many balls as possible within a 60- to 90-second time limit.
2. Add the pressure of a challenging opponent. The intensity of the challenge should increase from simply standing with the keeper to jumping with the keeper to legally charging the keeper.
3. Add a defender to increase the keeper's decision making and communication.
4. Add additional attackers and defenders as needed (2 v 1, 2 v 2, 3 v 2, 4 v 2, etc.).

AIR WARS

Group Exercise

Equipment   16 balls, marking disks, 2 goals (1 portable)

Organization   Construct a field 40 × 44 yards and divide the field in half, with a goal at each end. The two areas should be 20 × 44 yards. Organize four teams of players into two teams of 3 v 3 in each half. One team in each half defends, and the other attacks the goal. Have four servers position in the flank areas outside each half. Four more servers position behind the endlines on each side of the goals.

Procedure   If possible, goalkeepers are to safely box or palm all serves out of the playing area. The flank servers cross balls into the goal area, and endline servers chip or drive balls into the goal area. Servers would go in a set order. For example, flank servers in the first area would serve, followed by the flank servers in the opposite area. The two endline servers in one half would go, followed by the opposite endline servers. Flank servers cross balls within their half, but endline servers serve balls to the opposite half.

Attacking players attempt to score. Defending players attempt to clear the ball out of the area. Once either the keeper or a field player clears the ball out of the playing area, the next serve is taken.

Training Tips   Goalkeepers must be aggressive but should still decide which balls they can go for and which are out of range. This exercise is intended to force goalkeepers to extend their range with uncatchable balls.

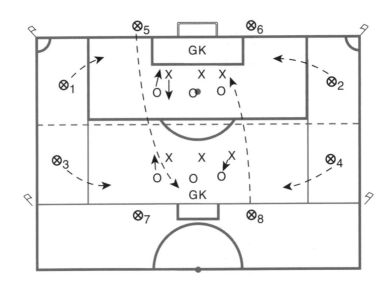

Variations

1. Have servers play a ball only when it goes out of play in their area (over the endline or touchline).
2. Allow the three defending players in one half to play with the three attacking players in the opposite half. For example, defending players may attempt to clear the ball out of the area or play to the attacking players in the other grid, including the opposite flank servers.
3. If a goalkeeper boxes a ball into the opposite area, it's a live ball for the attacking team.

5 v 5 + 2 CROSSING GAME

Team Exercise

Equipment   16 balls, marking disks, 2 goals (1 portable)

Organization   Set up the portable goal at the halfway line and create a penalty area with markers. Create a channel a few yards in from the touchline. Organize two teams of five field players, *but two players from each team must always be in the penalty area*. Each team also has two flank players in the channels, one on each side. Have balls supplied in both goals and with a coach at midfield.

Procedure   A coach starts the play at midfield. The object is for the possessing team to play a ball into the penalty area and challenge the goalkeeper. After any change of possession, players are restricted to play to one of the flank players before the goal can be attacked. The keeper restarts with a goal kick any ball that goes over the endline. The coach at midfield restarts any ball over the touchline. This ensures a free-flowing activity and manipulates the conditions of the exercise. Keepers can box or catch the crosses.

Training Tips   Goalkeepers must play aggressively, as they will always be challenged because of the presence of the two attacking players in the penalty area. In addition to the technical skills of boxing and catching crosses, keepers are also involved with the tactical decisions of organization and communication.

Variations
1. After they have crossed the ball, allow flank players to enter the field from their channel to create a numbers-up (6 v 5) situation.
2. Remove channels completely and simply play 6 v 6, still keeping two attacking players in the penalty area and still emphasizing crosses.

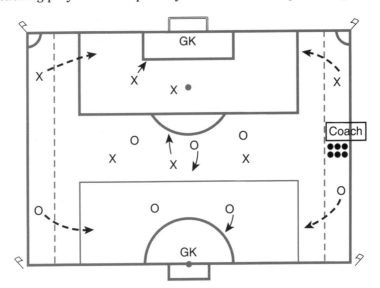

Diving to Save

The sight of a goalkeeper flying through the air with body fully extended is among the most exciting moments in a soccer match. Diving skills are as important to a keeper's success as they are pleasing to watch. Successful execution requires proper technique and timing coupled with the courage to leave your feet to make the save. Even though diving skills are a crowd favorite, they should never be used merely for show. Errors are likely to occur when sound goalkeeper tactics are replaced by unnecessary, attention-seeking acrobatics. The bottom line is that diving to save is really a last resort to use only when keepers can't get their body behind the ball. Still, such acrobatics can sometimes turn into heroics, and keepers do enjoy the challenge of making the big save. They also realize that the big save doesn't happen by chance. Diving is a finely honed skill mastered only through diligent training and endless repetition.

The crowd-pleasing, body-fully-extended, flying-through-the-air type of diving save actually occurs rarely over the course of a match. Although the keeper must be prepared to make such a save when needed, the majority of diving saves are much less spectacular, coming in the form of rolling balls, skipping balls, low-driven balls, swerving shots, dipping air balls, and point-blank reaction saves. These types of shots occur quite often, and the goalkeeper should be prepared to handle them. The more frequently a keeper performs a diving technique in training, the less likely he or she will have trouble handling a similar technique during a game. Multiple repetitions of diving skills enhance coordination of the feet, hands, and body and ultimately produce a more fluid execution of the technique. The psychological boost generated by rigorous game-simulated training also benefits the keeper.

Ground Balls

In most cases the goalkeeper can catch and hold a rolling ball of medium velocity arriving to his or her side. Two fundamental foot movements—the side shuffle and the collapse step—are essential for the proper execution of the dive. From the ready position, the keeper uses a side-shuffle movement to close the distance to the ball. When in position to leave his or her feet, the keeper pushes off with the foot farthest from the ball (e.g., push off the left foot when diving to the right). The left leg and arm follow to generate momentum in the direction of the dive. Simultaneously, the keeper executes a collapse step to quickly get the body to the ground. Keepers do this by stepping toward the ball with the right foot and then allowing the foot, ankle, and leg to collapse as they fall to one side (figure 5.1). A more detailed description of the side shuffle and collapse step foot movements can be found in chapter 8, Maximizing Footwork and Range.

The keeper aligns hands and head with the ball as it arrives and positions hands in a sideways version of the W, with fingers extended. The keeper receives the ball on the fingertips and palms, with the lower hand positioned behind the ball and elbow tucked to the side. The opposite (upper) hand comes down hard on top of the ball, pinning it to the ground. Proper positioning of the hands prevents the keeper from rolling onto his or her belly after making the save.

Low-Driven Balls

The keeper may not have time to shuffle sideways when diving to save a low-driven ball arriving with great velocity to his or her side. In such a situation, the keeper takes a short sideways power step with the foot nearest the ball and pushes off in the direction of the dive (see chapter 8). The opposite (upper) arm and leg follow to generate momentum in the direction of the dive. The keeper fully extends the lower arm and positions the hand behind the ball. The opposite (upper) hand comes down hard on top of the ball to pin it to the ground. Contact the ground on the side rather than on the belly. Diving on the side has several advantages: (1) the keeper's back is not exposed to an onrushing opponent, (2) the ball can be received employing the HEH principle, and (3) the risk of landing on top of the ball is reduced.

When unsure of holding the ball, keepers should follow this fundamental rule: when in doubt, parry it out! Rather than attempt to catch the ball, deflect it wide of the goal with the open palm of the lower hand. Angle the hand back slightly with wrist firm. An open palm contacts the inside half of the ball to deflect it wide of the post. The keeper should not

Figure 5.1 Using the collapse dive for a rolling ball.

position the hand directly behind the ball, as this may cause the ball to rebound outward in front of the goal.

Diving for Low Balls

1. Begin in the ready position.
2. Shuffle sideways to close the distance to the ball.
3. Execute the collapse step to go to the ground for a rolling ball of medium velocity.
4. Execute the power step to vault sideways to save a low-driven ball of great velocity.
5. The opposite arm and leg follow to generate momentum in the direction of the dive.
6. Tuck elbow to side when going to the ground.
7. Pin the ball to the ground, lower hand behind, upper hand on top.
8. Parry any shot that might be tough to hold.
9. Recover quickly if the ball is not deflected out of play.
10. Always dive forward to attack the ball. Never dive backward.

Air Balls

With a few minor exceptions, the techniques used when diving to save low balls also apply when saving shots traveling above ground. Keepers should use a quick side-shuffle step followed by a collapse step when diving to save a ball arriving to their immediate side. When the ball is farther away, it becomes necessary to use a power step rather than the collapse step (see chapter 8). To execute the power step, the keeper takes a short, sideways step with the foot nearest the ball. He or she flexes at the knee with the foot angled so that toes point in the direction of the dive. Push off the lead foot while simultaneously vaulting the opposite leg upward. The opposite (upper) arm follows in a powerful whip-like motion along a path up and over the head. The opposite arm should not thrust across the body, as that motion shortens the dive by pulling the body down toward the ground. The body should fully extend parallel to the ground as hands contact the ball (figure 5.2). Upon catching the ball, the keeper's focus shifts to landing properly. The ball should contact the ground, first followed by the forearm, shoulder, hip, and leg, in that order. Tuck the elbow (lower arm) to the side; otherwise the ball might be jarred

Figure 5.2 Using the power step to catch an air ball.

loose when the body contacts the ground. Pin the ball to the ground with legs extended behind and positioned in a sideways V, and then pull the ball to the chest.

KEY ELEMENTS OF PEAK PERFORMANCE

Diving for Air Balls

1. Begin in the ready position.
2. Initiate movement with a power step in direction of dive.
3. Push off with the foot nearest the ball.
4. Thrust the opposite arm (farthest from the ball) upward and over the head to generate momentum in direction of the dive.
5. Extend arms and catch the ball on fingertips.
6. Contact the ground in this sequence: ball, forearm, shoulder, hip, legs.
7. Parry a ball that cannot be held.
8. Attack the ball by diving to the ball. Never fall or dive backward.

The Reaction Save

When faced with a point-blank shot to either side, the keeper will not have time to think about proper footwork, correct technique, coordinated body movement, or much else for that matter. In such a situation, he or she must get parallel to the ground immediately and attempt to deflect the ball wide of or over the top of the goal. The reaction save is typically accomplished using one of the following techniques:

- The open palm deflects both low and high shots.
- The flat surface of a closed fist deflects high shots over the goal.
- The heel of the hand (with fist closed) deflects low shots wide of the goal

Diving Drills

Diving skills should be taught progressively and safely. The age and level of the goalkeeper determines appropriate training intensity. Younger, inexperienced goalkeepers should master the fundamental movements before the demands of training are increased significantly. We also recommend conducting all diving drills in safe areas. Goalkeepers don't become tougher by training on rough or rocky ground; they become injured.

When possible, conduct diving drills on a soft grassy area of the field. Some training facilities even have diving pits designed for goalkeeper training. The pits are filled with sand, sawdust, or foam pads to provide a soft training surface; this allows the keeper to focus on technique without fear of injury.

Limit diving practice to short, intense bursts of activity. Requiring the goalkeeper to make too many dives in succession defeats the purpose of the drill, and the objective of improving technique will not be met. Although keeper training should be physically and mentally challenging, it should not be viewed as an endurance contest. To achieve the desired results, practice should be demanding but fun. The first four individual drills on the following pages are for ground balls; the next three are for air balls.

FUNDAMENTAL DIVING

Individual Exercise

Equipment   2 balls

Organization   Two goalkeepers kneel facing one another. Place a ball to the immediate right and left of each keeper.

Procedure   On command, both keepers fall to their right and pin the ball to the ground using the hands-eyes-head (HEH) technique. Keepers immediately return to a kneeling position and repeat to the opposite side. Continue for 30 to 40 seconds, then rest and repeat the exercise.

Training Tips   Arm motion is important. The opposite arm, farthest from the ball, should be thrust up and behind the head to generate momentum in the direction of the dive.

Variations

1. Same organization, but keepers begin from a squat position. Balls are placed three to four yards further out.
2. The keeper starts from ready position. Balls are positioned four to six yards out. The keeper takes a collapse step to pin the ball to the ground.

RECEIVING ROLLING BALLS

Individual Exercise

Equipment   2 to 3 balls

Organization   The goalkeeper, kneeling, faces a server at a distance of five yards; the server rolls the ball to either side of the keeper.

Procedure   The keeper falls to his or her side and pins the ball to the ground using the HEH technique. Keepers immediately return to a kneeling position and repeat to the same side. Initially, they dive to the same side to ensure correct technique by maintaining a rhythm. Continue for 30 to 40 seconds, then rest, and repeat the exercise going to the other side.

Training Tips   The keeper dives efficiently and should not dive over the ball. It's important to dive directly toward the ball. Do not dive backward. Always attack the ball. The motion of the opposite arm is still important.

Variations

1. Same organization but keepers begin from a squat position.
2. The goalkeeper starts from ready position. The goalkeeper should take a collapse step to pin the ball to the ground.
3. Progress to alternating sides after each serve.
4. React to the serve, having the server change sides.

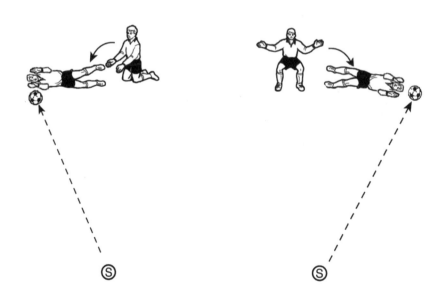

SHUFFLE AND SAVE

Individual Exercise

Equipment   4 to 6 balls, 1 regulation goal

Organization   A server stands eight yards front and center of the goal. There are cones or flags one to two yards out from each post and one to two yards inside each post. The goalkeeper stands on one post.

Procedure   The goalkeeper shuffles across the goal area. The server plays a ball toward the marker. The keeper must shuffle over and save the ball before it goes behind the cone or flag. The keeper gets up and shuffles to the opposite side for another save. Continue for 30 to 40 seconds.

Training Tips   The purpose of the markers is to get the goalkeeper to dive forward to the ball, as opposed to diving backward. The keeper should use proper footwork across the goal and a correct collapse step to pin the ball to the ground.

Variations

1. Start the goalkeeper in the center of the goal. The server varies the serve to either side.
2. Increase the pace of the serve, forcing the keeper to deflect the ball around the marker and the goalpost.

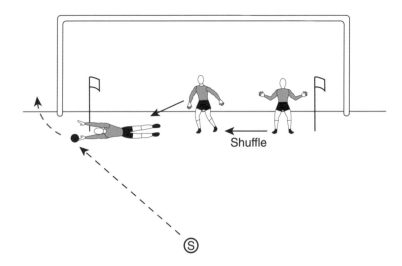

THREE-GOAL GAME

Individual Exercise

Equipment   4 to 6 balls, 6 cones or flags

Organization   Set up three goals a few yards apart. A server is in front of the goals, and the goalkeeper is behind them.

Procedure   The server calls out or points to one of the goals, and the keeper sprints to that goal to make the save. Pace serves so the goalkeeper can get to the ball, take a collapse step, and hold on to the ball. After each save, the keeper should immediately get up and return to start position. Continue 30 to 40 seconds, rest, and repeat.

Training Tips   After sprinting to the ball, the goalkeeper focuses on getting his or her body balanced and under control to ensure a proper collapse step to the ball. The keeper should attempt to hold every shot. This exercise also forces the keeper to dive forward toward the ball.

Variations

1. Increase velocity of the serve so that the keeper has to deflect shots around the flag or cone.
2. Have the keeper start from various positions (face down on the ground, sitting, lying on his or her back, lying on side, etc.) before getting up and going to the goal.
3. Have the keeper do a forward roll before entering the goal to make the save.

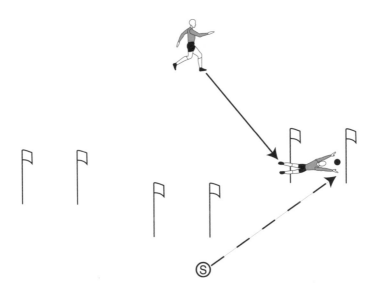

FUNDAMENTAL FLYING

Individual Exercise

Equipment   2 to 4 balls, cones, small hurdles or plyometric device

Organization   The goalkeeper starts the exercise in a squatting position facing a server four to six yards away.

Procedure   The server tosses a high ball to the keeper's side, forcing him or her to vault in the air and make the save. The serves should be to the same side during the first attempts of this exercise. Repeat these tosses for 30 to 40 seconds. Rest and serve to the other side.

Training Tips   The goalkeeper focuses on catching the ball and using proper motion of the opposite arm and leg to generate momentum toward the ball. The keeper should attempt to land with the ball touching the ground first, followed by the forearms, shoulders, hips, and legs.

Variations

1. Alternate serves to each side.
2. The goalkeeper stands in "ready" position with the server six yards away. The server tosses an air ball to the keeper's side so that he or she must take a power step when diving to save.
3. Place an obstacle (a ball, cones, small hurdle, etc.) next to the goalkeeper's feet. The keeper must take a power step over the obstacle to catch the serve.
4. The goalkeeper takes a few shuffles before vaulting over the obstacle and making the save.
5. A goal is set up using cones or flags. The keeper stands to the side of the goal, and the server is in front of the goal. The goalkeeper must shuffle to the goal, take a power step, and vault out to catch an air ball served toward the goal.

DEFLECTING (PARRYING) TECHNIQUE

Individual Exercise

Equipment   2 to 4 balls, cones or flags

Organization   The goalkeeper begins in a squatting position. A server holds a ball in each hand with arms outstretched, facing the keeper at a distance of one yard. A third player is next to the server to supply balls.

Procedure   The server tosses one of the balls to the keeper's side. The keeper quickly reacts to deflect the ball with the open palm of the upper hand. The server alternates tossing to the keeper's right and left. Repeat these serves for 30 to 40 seconds, rest, and repeat.

Training Tips   The keeper quickly pushes off and explodes to the ball. Tosses should be out of the keeper's reach. The keeper uses the open palm of the upper hand to direct the ball out and away from the server.

Variations

1. Add a cone or, preferably, a flag several yards to the keeper's side. When the keeper deflects the serve, he or she focuses on attempting to direct the ball around and behind the flag, which simulates a goalpost.
2. The server serves the ball toward the ground, forcing the keeper to deflect around the flag with the lower hand.
3. The keeper stands in a ready position to start the exercise and must return to start position after each serve.

REACTION SAVES

Individual Exercise

Equipment   6 to 8 balls, 2 regulation goals (or 4 cones or flags)

Organization   Place the two goals about 10 yards apart, facing each other. A server positions between the goals, facing a player across from the server and standing between the goals. Position a goalkeeper in each goal.

Procedure   The server tosses an easy serve to the player, who strikes a volley first time to either goal. The keeper makes a reaction save on a first-time, point-blank volley. Continue for 90 seconds.

Training Tips   The keeper is in ready position, set to explode to the ball. The keeper tries to hold the ball if possible but to deflect it wide of the goal if it can't be held.

Variations

1. The server plays a ground ball to the shooter to give the keeper a different look and reaction.
2. The shooter can head the ball as well as volley it.
3. Have the server or the shooter attempt to play the rebounds.

KEEPER VS. KEEPER

Group Exercise

Equipment   6 to 8 balls, 2 full-size goals (1 portable)

Organization   Position two goals 20 yards apart with a keeper in each goal.

Procedure   One keeper has a ball and is allowed to shoot, volley, or throw the ball into the opposing goal. The keeper with the ball may take two to four steps while holding the ball (depending on the level), or one to three touches if a shot. The defending keeper advances off the line to narrow the angle and make the save. Any ball rebounding in front of the goal is a live ball. Keepers alternate shooting at each other. Play to a set number of goals, awarding a point for each goal, or use a time limit.

Training Tips   Emphasize competitiveness and finding ways to keep the ball out of the goal. See variation 1 if you want to emphasize technique.

Variations

1. The defending goalkeeper is awarded two points for cleanly holding any shot and one point for any deflection placed wide of the goal and out of play.
2. A second player is added to each team as a designated shooter. After each save or restart, the keeper plays a ball to his or her teammate, who is permitted only one touch before shooting.

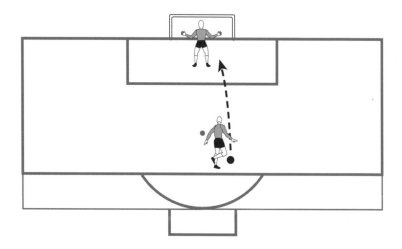

ALL VS. KEEPER

Group Exercise

Equipment   4 to 6 balls, one portable central goal or flags

Organization   A portable goal (or two flags) is positioned in the center of a field 30 × 40 yards. A neutral goalkeeper positions to defend the goal. Two teams are chosen, preferably 4 v 4 or 5 v 5.

Procedure   Play a regular game except that the players are permitted to score from either side of the central goal. The keeper constantly readjusts position in relation to the ball. Teams are awarded a point for each score, and the keeper is awarded a point for each save. After each save, the keeper distributes to a coach, who restarts play.

Training Tips   Because this drill requires the keeper to make many kinds of saves it is quite demanding. A second or third keeper should be available, with rotation occurring every few minutes. To emphasize diving, use variation 1. To emphasize fitness and footwork, use variation 2.

Variations

1. Place an eight-yard square around the goal, so all attempts on goal must be shots. Players are only permitted inside this square after a rebound.
2. Prohibit the keeper from going to the other side of the goal by going between the posts. The keeper must go *around* the post or the flags to defend the other side of the goal.

TRIANGLE EXERCISE

Group Exercise

Equipment   4 to 6 balls, 3 flags

Organization   Place three flags in a triangle eight yards apart. Place a server with a ball five yards from each side, facing the triangle. The keeper should be in ready position, facing the first server.

Procedure   The keeper shuffles first to the right around the triangle goal. Each server serves to the keeper's right, forcing him or her to stretch to make a save. After the keeper saves the first serve, he or she gets up to his or her feet and shuffles around the next flag for the next serve. Continue for 30 to 40 seconds, rest, and repeat going the opposite way. Servers should serve ground balls or air balls at first.

Training Tips   The keeper springs to his or her feet as quickly as possible and shuffles around the flag to the next server. The keeper tries to catch and hold all serves or to deflect them around the flag if the ball can't be held. The keeper uses proper shuffling footwork.

Variations

1. Servers pick up the velocity of the serve and force the keeper to stretch the body completely.

2. Alternate servers so that the keeper must change direction and go to a different side of the triangle.

3. Play 4 v 4 or 5 v 5 with two goalkeepers in the triangle goal. Either team can score through any side of the goal. The coach dictates which goalkeeper covers two sides of the goal and which keeper covers only one side.

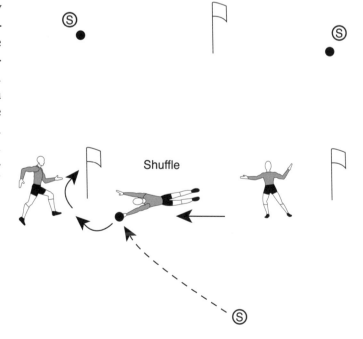

Shuffle

ANGLE SHOOTING

Group Exercise

Equipment   2 regulation goals (1 portable), markers, 16 balls

Organization   Two goals face each other 24 yards apart. The field should be 16 × 24 yards and divided into three sections. The sections in front of the goal are about 6 × 16, with a 12 × 16 middle section. The middle section has a 2 v 2 with one neutral player to create a 3 v 2. Four players station outside the playing area, one each near the six-yard lines. Thus, each team has two perimeter players shooting to their goal. The keeper must stay in the six-yard area. The coach positions outside the playing area with a supply of balls.

Procedure   The coach starts the game by playing to the players in the middle grid. The attacking players may shoot or pass to the perimeter players going to their goal for a shot. Players can only enter the goalkeeper's six-yard area for a rebound. Any rebound is a live ball. The coach restarts the game after the ball goes out of bounds or a goal is scored.

Training Tips   Attacking players should be encouraged to take open shots. If they are not open for a shot, they pass to perimeter players on their team for a shot. The perimeter players provide the keeper with shots from various angles, forcing the keeper to constantly adjust position.

Variations
1. Add an extra neutral player to create a 4 v 2 in the middle.
2. Widen or narrow the field (depending on the ability of the players).

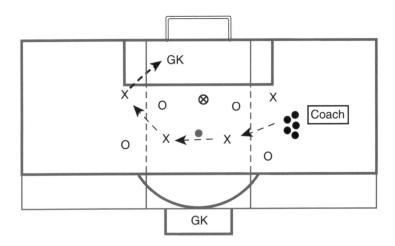

5 v 2 + 5 v 2 (7 v 7)

Team Exercise

Equipment 2 regulation goals (1 portable), markers, 16 balls

Organization The field is 44 × 60 yards and divided in half. Only two defending players are allowed in each half, creating a 5 v 2 in a 30 × 44 grid. Balls are placed in both goals.

Procedure Keepers start each play with a throw or kick to their teammates in the attacking half. Attacking players are permitted only one or two touches before they must shoot or pass. If defenders or the keeper get the ball, they immediately play to their teammates in the attacking half of the field.

Training Tips Attacking players are encouraged to shoot. The keeper needs to constantly adjust positioning and to communicate to the defenders. Accurate distribution is important.

Variations

1. Restrict the attacking players to only one pass before they must shoot.
2. Modify the numbers. For example, allow a defender to move into the attacking zone to create a 6 v 2, or allow an extra defender to move into the defending zone to create a 5 v 3.

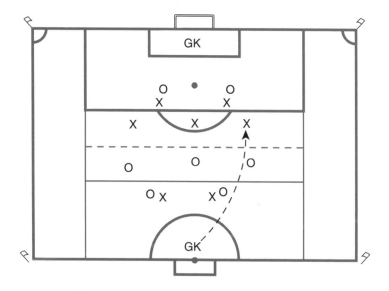

Saving the Breakaway

An opponent with the ball who has broken free of the last defender provides the ultimate one-on-one test for the goalkeeper. Breakaways develop from various angles and involve players of different dribbling skills and running speeds, so it's difficult to provide a standard technique for making the big save. In all cases there is very little margin for error. A combination of timing, technique, and courage is crucial for the goalkeeper to succeed. Several fundamental principles true of all breakaway situations will improve chances of making the save. It's imperative to maintain balance and body control when advancing to initiate a challenge. Recklessly charging forward in an attempt to intimidate the player with the ball usually results in a goal scored or, even worse, injury to the keeper, the opponent, or both. When closing the distance to the ball, the keeper shifts into a semi-crouch position. In preparation to save, he or she must anticipate when the opponent will release the ball. Making the right judgment depends largely on the keeper's ability to read the game. The keeper must quickly analyze the situation and sense when to come off the line, how fast to come off, at what angle, at what body position, and most important, when to go down to the ground to make the save. Poor decisions result in poor goalkeeping.

There's no substitute for a high level of technical ability. The more proficient a keeper becomes at performing the skills used in breakaways, the more likely he or she will make the save and maintain possession of the ball. Proper technique also reduces risk of injury.

Narrowing the Angle

Once an opponent has clearly broken free of the last defender, the keeper moves forward to narrow the shooting angle. When advancing toward the ball, he or she shifts from the upright ready position into a semi-crouch posture (figure 6.1a). From a crouch position (figure 6.1b), the keeper can

Figure 6.1 In *(a)* semi-crouch position and *(b)* crouch position, advancing toward the ball.

go to the ground more quickly. The lower center of gravity will also enable him or her to change direction more easily. Speed of approach depends on the situation. When the opponent has pushed the ball several yards ahead so that it's not under close control, the keeper moves forward quickly. When the opponent has the ball under close control, the keeper's advance is slower and more cautious. Balance and body control should be maintained at all times. The keeper needs to dictate the movements of the opponent (not vice versa!) by approaching at an angle that forces the opponent to dribble diagonally away from (wide of) the goal. This shifts the advantage to the keeper, reducing the shooting angle and exposing less of the goal. If the dribbler can be prevented from cutting the ball back toward the center of the goal, he or she will have a much tougher shooting angle with less of the goal open.

Going to the Ground

The most critical factor in making the save in a breakaway situation is the keeper's ability to go to the ground at precisely the best moment to smother the ball. The keeper must analyze the dribbler's body movements, anticipate when the ball will be released, and then go to the ground at one of the following moments: (a) an instant before the shot is released while the ball is still at the dribbler's feet, (b) just as the ball is released, or (c) when there is separation between the ball and the opponent, allowing the ball to be smothered before the dribbler can regain control. Going to the ground too early, before the opponent has committed to one action, or too late, after the shot has been released, usually results in a goal scored.

The keeper shifts into a semi-crouch position while closing the distance to the ball; arms extend down to the sides, palms are forward, and fingers nearly touch the ground. The keeper goes to the ground on his or her side to make the save, midsection aligned with the ball (figure 6.2). Arms and hands are positioned to cover the near post side of the goal; legs extend in the opposite direction to protect the far post area. From this position, the keeper can quickly scramble up onto hands and knees to cover the ball if the opponent attempts to push it past (toward the flank). If the dribbler cuts the ball back toward the center of the goal, the keeper uses legs and feet to kick the ball away.

Pinning the Ball

The keeper extends arms and hands to pin the ball rather than allowing it to come into his or her body. Both hands are brought down with force, the bottom hand behind the ball and the upper hand on top to prevent a rebound (figure 6.3). The keeper remains on his or her side when making

Figure 6.2 Going to the ground, with hands stretched out making the save.

the save. Rolling onto the belly increases risk of injury by exposing the back and kidneys to a hard-charging opponent. Once the ball is secured, it's immediately pulled to the chest.

Making the big save in a breakaway situation requires courage and determination. The play is not always over nor the battle lost if the keeper fails to secure the ball cleanly on the first attempt. Simply forcing the opponent into a poorer shooting angle might make him or her push the ball wide of the goal. At the very least it provides another attempt at pinning the ball.

KEY ELEMENTS OF PEAK PERFORMANCE

Saving the Breakaway

1. Initiate movement from the ready (upright) position.
2. Move forward quickly when the ball is not under close control of the dribbler.
3. Move forward cautiously when the ball is close to the dribbler's feet.
4. Shift into semi-crouch with arms extended down, palms forward, and fingertips brushing the ground beside your feet.
5. Anticipate the shot.
6. Go to the ground on your side to obstruct as much of the goal as possible.
7. Position arms and hands to cover the near post area of the goal; position feet and legs to protect the central and far post areas.

Figure 6.3 Pinning the ball.

8. Extend arms and pin the ball to the ground with one hand behind and one on top.
9. Remain on side after making the save.

Breakaway Drills

Saving a breakaway is among the most difficult challenges facing the goal-keeper, with very little margin for error. Training for the breakaway is equally challenging. It's best to strike a balance between hard, intense one-on-one confrontations and common sense—yes, you want to prac-tice to simulate game situations, but an injured goalkeeper is hardly in the team's best interests. That said, when training to save the breakaway, there's no way the keeper can avoid going to the ground—it's simply part of the deal. The technique must be practiced often and performed ag-gressively. It's the coach's responsibility to get the keeper plenty of rep-etitions while avoiding unnecessary wear and tear on the body. Doing so requires preparation and planning. Conducting breakaway drills in safe (no glass or metal objects, etc.), soft, grassy areas minimizes risk of in-jury and enables the keeper to benefit from training exercises. Field play-ers involved in breakaway exercises should create competitive situations for the goalkeeper while maintaining balance and body control at all times, thus avoiding collisions with the keeper. The focus of training for inexpe-rienced goalkeepers should be on technique, with minimal pressure from an opponent. Only after fundamental techniques are mastered is it safe to progress to pressure and gamelike conditions.

BREAKDOWN FUNDAMENTALS

Individual Exercise

Equipment   2 balls

Organization   Two to four goalkeepers face each other at a distance of about 20 yards.

Procedure   Goalkeeper A dribbles toward Goalkeeper B. Keeper B advances toward the dribbler, breaks down to a crouch position, and goes to the ground to smother the ball. Keeper B then puts the ball to her or his feet and dribbles to Keeper C, who also breaks down and smothers the ball. Continue until each keeper makes 10 saves.

Training Tips   The goalkeeper starts from a standing position, advances under control, step for step with the dribbler, and slowly breaks down to a crouch position. Once in a crouch position, the keeper goes to one side, making a long barrier, and goes hands first to the ball. The keeper dribbling the ball should dribble at the goalkeeper and allow the keeper to make the save.

Variations

1. Goalkeepers in a crouch position place a stationary ball to each side. The keeper then collapses to the ball, gets up, and goes to the other side. Continue for 30 seconds, then rest and repeat.

2. Two servers are on either side of the goalkeeper, about five yards away. The goalkeeper starts from a standing position and advances to the server, who dribbles to the keeper. The keeper breaks down and smothers the ball. The keeper immediately springs to his or her feet and prepares to save the ball from the other server, who dribbles to the keeper's other side. Continue for 30 seconds, with dribblers alternating sides so that the keeper goes down on each side.

NARROWING THE ANGLE

Group Exercise

Equipment 5 to 10 balls, 1 regulation goal

Organization Three to five servers, each with a ball, position at various angles and distances in the penalty area away from the goal. The keeper is in the goal.

Procedure The coach directs one server to dribble toward the goal. The keeper advances to the server, breaks down, and smothers the ball. After this save, the goalkeeper returns to starting position in the goal. The process continues with a different server selected by the coach. Initially, servers should only try to dribble around the keeper. Continue the exercise for 60 seconds.

Training Tips The keeper advances stride for stride with the server and breaks down to a crouch position to make the save. As soon as one save is made, the keeper jumps to his or her feet and sprints back to a good starting position in the goal. The servers wait for the keeper to get back to starting position before the next dribbler advances.

Variations

1. Servers dribble close to the keeper and attempt to pass the ball under the keeper, forcing him or her to get to the ground quickly. The keeper times the approach to get to the ground either just as the ball is shot or right after the shot.

2. The server can take the opportunity to shoot earlier.

3. The server can pass to another player who then advances to the goal. The keeper must recover laterally and then advance to the next server.

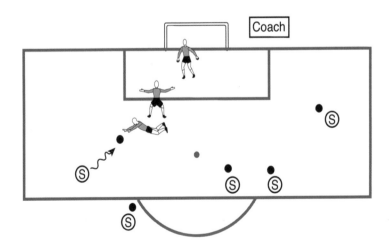

READING THE THROUGH BALL

Group Exercise

Equipment   6 to 8 balls, 1 regulation goal

Organization   A server positions 35 yards from the goal, with a line of attackers positioned at each side.

Procedure   The server passes the ball ahead to the attacker, who receives the ball at top speed and dribbles to the goal on a breakaway. Allow the keeper to return to starting position after each save attempt and repeat the exercise to the other side. The keeper takes six serves, three to each side, before alternating with another keeper.

Training Tips   The keeper may advance when the ball is played and should have a realistic starting position. The server varies the pace and distance of the pass, attempting to place passes both inside and outside the penalty area.

Variations

1. The second line of players may become a recovering defender, forcing the keeper to read the ball, the attacker, and the defender.
2. Add a third line, two attacking lines, and one defending line. This creates a 2 v 1 breakaway and forces the keeper to deal with a second attacker.

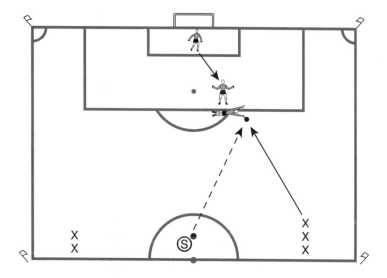

BREAKAWAY CITY

Group Exercise

Equipment   2 goals (1 portable), 6 to 8 balls, disk markers

Organization   Construct a field 20 × 24 yards divided into thirds. Play 2 v 2 with two neutral attacking players to create a 4 v 2. The coach starts each play outside the middle third with a supply of balls.

Procedure   Players can shoot only from within the attack third of the field and cannot enter the attack third of the field ahead of the ball. Play 3- to 5-minute games.

Training Tips   Players are encouraged to dribble directly to goal, with minimal passing. The coach manipulates the exercise by restarting each play and setting up breakaway opportunities.

Variation   Play 2 v 2 + 1 (3 v 2) inside the playing area, but place two neutral players outside. When the ball is played to the neutral players, they immediately dribble to the goal.

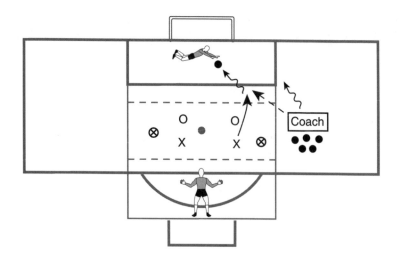

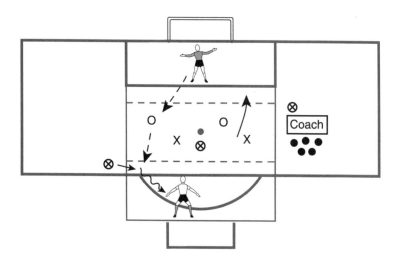

BREAKAWAY GAME

Team Exercise

Equipment   2 regulation goals and disk markers, 4 to 6 balls

Organization   Play on a full field. Place markers across the field 30 yards from both goals to create three sections of the field. Place balls in each goal.

Procedure   Begin by playing 5 v 5 with two neutral attacking players in the middle section of the field. No player is allowed in the attack third of the field *before* the ball. The team in possession of the ball attempts to score either by dribbling into the attack third or by playing a penetrating pass. Either circumstance should create a breakaway situation.

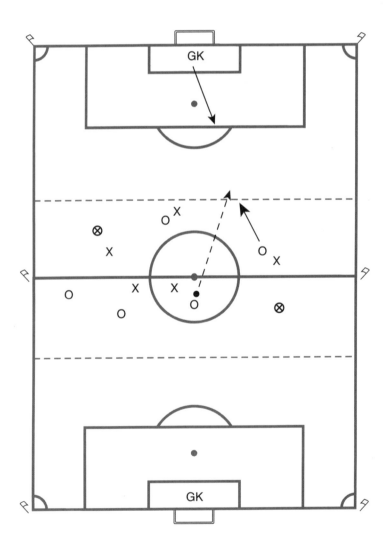

Training Tips   The goalkeeper must control the final defending third of the field and needs to stay connected to his or her defenders by maintaining a realistic starting position. Players should be encouraged to find ways to penetrate into the attack third. Once the goalkeeper gains possession of the ball, the defending team drops to the middle third of the field.

Variations

1. Restrict players to play one- or two-touch soccer in the middle section to ensure more penetration with a pass.
2. Modify organization of the teams according to the skill level of your team. An example would be to add more neutrals (4 v 4 + 4) to ensure more attacks. If the coach is more concerned with communication and the goalkeeper staying connected with the defenders, eliminate the neutral players and play 6 v 6 to make the exercise more realistic.
3. Eliminate markers and have defenders step up to compact the defense and create offside traps. Use coaches or extra players to call offside.

Distributing the Ball

The goalkeeper's responsibilities do not end once the save has been made. Through accurate distribution of the ball, the keeper also plays an integral role in transition from team defense to team attack. Common methods of distribution include rolling, throwing, and kicking (see chart on page 118). Keepers should be comfortable with each technique, as they will probably use them all at one time or another. To choose the best method of distribution for a given situation, consider the guidelines below.

• **Choose accuracy over distance.** In most situations, a short outlet pass played accurately to a teammate's feet is preferable to kicking the ball as high and far as possible down the field.

• **Vary the delivery.** The keeper should keep opponents guessing as to where, when, and to whom the ball will be released. The ebb and flow of the game usually dictates the choice of options. Some situations warrant immediate distribution of the ball, while in others it's better to delay for a few moments to slow the pace and settle the team.

• **Change the point of attack.** Distribute the ball into an area where a teammate has ample time and space to receive and control it. The side of the field opposite the position of the ball is usually available for a quick outlet pass. For example, after receiving a ball crossed from the left flank (opponent's right), the keeper immediately looks to outlet the ball to a teammate on the right flank. The ball should not be distributed to a player who will be put under immediate pressure from a challenging opponent, particularly if that player is positioned within the defending third of the field nearest the goal.

• **Support the outlet pass.** Recent FIFA rule changes permit keepers to take as many steps with the ball as they want to, provided the ball is released into play within six seconds after securing it. In most cases, the keeper will have enough time to run forward to the edge of the penalty box before releasing the ball. After distributing the ball, the keeper moves into a support position to be available for a return pass. Note that FIFA rules stipulate that a ball deliberately passed back to the keeper must be controlled and played with the feet, not the hands. For this reason it is essential that the keeper become comfortable playing the ball with his or her feet.

Rolling the Ball

Rolling is an effective method of distributing the ball accurately over distances of 20 yards or less. The rolling motion is similar to that used when bowling. The keeper faces the target with the ball cupped in the palm of the throwing hand (figure 7.1a), steps toward the target with the foot opposite the throwing arm, bends forward at the waist, and releases the ball at ground level with a bowling-type motion (figure 7.1b). Rolling the ball is most appropriate when playing on a dry, flat field surface. Use caution when the field surface is rough or weather conditions are poor, as the ball may not roll true to form.

Figure 7.1 Rolling the ball: *(a)* with ball in hand and *(b)* after release.

Distribution by Rolling

1. Face the target with shoulders squared.
2. Hold the ball in the palm of the hand.
3. Step toward target with the leg opposite the throwing arm.
4. Bend forward at the waist and release ball at ground level with a bowling-type motion.
5. Keep head steady with vision focused on target.
6. Use a smooth follow-through motion of the throwing arm.

Throwing the Ball

The goalkeeper can distribute the ball over longer distances by throwing it. He or she has the option of three throwing techniques, usually depending on keeper ability and on the distance of the target from the keeper. The *sidearm throw* is generally used to distribute the ball over short- and medium-range distances. The greatest benefits of the sidearm toss are ease of release and a high degree of accuracy. The *baseball throw* technique is used to toss the ball over medium and long distances. The *javelin throw* is used to heave the ball over long distances when accuracy is not as important as distance.

Sidearm Throw

To perform the sidearm throw, the keeper angles the body sideways (the shoulder of the nonthrowing arm pointed toward the target) and draws back the throwing arm with elbow bent 90 degrees (figure 7.2a). He or she holds the ball at about shoulder height in the palm of the hand and steps toward the target with the leg opposite the throwing arm, swinging the throwing arm forward on a slightly downward plane with slight flexion at the knee. The ball is released about waist high (figure 7.2b). The wrist snaps forward and downward to generate a spin on the ball, which causes the ball to skim along the ground toward the target.

Sidearm Throw

1. Angle body toward target.
2. Hold the ball in the palm of the hand at about shoulder height with elbow bent.
3. Step toward target with the foot opposite the throwing hand.

Figure 7.2 Sidearm throw: *(a)* with ball in hand and *(b)* after release.

4. Perform the throwing motion along a slightly downward plane.
5. Release the ball at waist height.
6. Snap the wrist downward as ball is released.
7. Put spin on the ball.

Baseball Throw

The baseball throw is used to distribute the ball accurately over distances of 25 to 40 yards. It's not a good option for younger keepers who lack upper body and arm strength. The throwing motion is similar to that used when pitching a baseball. The keeper holds the ball about head high in the palm of the hand, with the elbow flexed about 90 degrees (figure 7.3a). He or she steps toward the target with the foot opposite the throwing arm and uses an overhand throwing motion with a complete follow-through. The wrist snaps forward as the ball is released (figure 7.3b).

Figure 7.3 Baseball throw: *(a)* with ball in hand and *(b)* after release.

KEY ELEMENTS OF PEAK PERFORMANCE

Baseball Throw

1. Angle body sideways to target.
2. Hold the ball in the palm of the hand.
3. Cock the throwing arm with the ball held behind the ear.
4. Extend the opposite arm toward the target.
5. Step toward the target with the foot opposite the throwing arm.
6. Use a three-quarter or overhand throwing motion.
7. Snap the wrist toward the target as the ball is released.
8. Use a complete follow-through.

Javelin Throw

The javelin throw is used to distribute the ball over distances of 40 yards or greater. As a rule, this method provides less accuracy than the side-arm or baseball throw, although professional keepers can usually put the ball just about where they want it. The keeper executes the javelin throw by curling the hand around the ball, encasing the ball within the fingers, palm, and wrist about waist high. The throwing arm extends behind the body; the upper body arches back (figure 7.4a). The nonthrowing arm extends forward and points toward the target. The throwing motion travels along an upward arc and concludes with a whiplike motion of the arm above the head (figure 7.4b). The ball is released at any point along the throwing arc, depending on the trajectory desired. The sooner the ball is released along the arc, the higher the trajectory. Releasing the ball near the completion of the throwing motion makes the ball travel nearly parallel to the ground.

Figure 7.4 Javelin throw: *(a)* with ball in hand and *(b)* after release.

Javelin Throw

1. Encase the ball within the fingers and palm, with wrist cocked.
2. Extend the throwing arm behind the body, with body angled sideways to target.
3. Extend the opposite arm toward the target.
4. Arch the upper body back with ball held at waist level.
5. Keep head steady.
6. Step toward the target.
7. Use a whiplike motion of the throwing arm to generate maximum distance on the throw.
8. Release the ball at some point along the throwing arc.

Kicking the Ball

Although less accurate than throwing, kicking is effective to send the ball into the opponent's half of the field. Three kicking techniques are available to the goalkeeper, depending on the situation. The *full-volley punt* and *half-volley punt* (dropkick) are used to distribute the ball once the save has been made and the ball is securely in the goalkeeper's hands. The primary advantage of a punt or dropkick is that the ball is immediately sent into the opposite half of the field, a tactic that prevents the opposing team from consolidating its players behind the ball to compact the space. The *instep kick* is used to distribute the ball off the ground after it has been played back to the goalkeeper by a teammate or to return a ball into play that traveled over the endline and was last touched by an opponent.

Full-Volley Punt

The keeper executes the full-volley punt by standing erect with shoulders square to the target and arms extended in front. He or she holds the ball about waist high in the palm of the hand opposite the kicking foot, keeping the head steady and eyes focused on the ball (figure 7.5a). The keeper then steps forward with the nonkicking foot, releases the ball (figure 7.5b), and volleys it directly out of the air using a complete follow-through motion of the kicking leg. Shoulders and hips are squared to the target. The kicking foot is fully extended and firmly positioned as the instep contacts the center of the ball.

Figure 7.5 Full volley punt: *(a)* with ball in hand and *(b)* after release.

Half-Volley Punt (Dropkick)

The dropkick—an effective alternative to the full-volley punt—is a particularly good option on windy days, as the trajectory of the ball is lower and more direct than with a full-volley punt. The kicking mechanics are similar to the full-volley punt except that foot contact with the ball occurs at the instant the ball contacts the ground, rather than directly out of the air. The keeper stands erect with the ball, about waist level, in the palm of the hand opposite the kicking foot. Some keepers prefer to hold the ball in both hands. In either case, the keeper steps forward with the nonkicking foot to release the ball. He or she then draws back the kicking leg with the foot fully extended and firmly positioned (figure 7.6) and drives the instep of the kicking foot through the center of the ball at the moment the ball contacts the ground. Lean back slightly to get loft on the serve. Shoulders and hips remain squared to the target. There is a complete follow-through motion of the kicking leg.

Figure 7.6 Half volley punt.

KEY ELEMENTS OF PEAK PERFORMANCE

Full-Volley and Half-Volley Punts

1. Extend arms and hold ball in palm of hand opposite the kicking foot.
2. Square shoulders and hips with target.
3. Keep head steady with vision on ball.
4. Step forward with nonkicking (balance) foot.
5. Draw back the kicking leg with knee flexed.
6. Extend and firmly position the kicking foot.
7. Drive the instep through the center of the ball.
8. Use a complete follow-through motion.

Instep Kick

The instep drive technique is used to serve the ball along the ground or through the air over a long distance. The keeper approaches from behind the ball, at a slight angle. Shoulders and hips are squared to the intended target. To play the ball along the ground, the keeper plants the balance foot (nonkicking foot) beside the ball and drives the instep through the center of the ball with toes pointed down and foot firm (figure 7.7a). The knee of the kicking leg is directly above the ball at the moment of foot contact. To serve the ball through the air, the keeper plants the balance foot slightly behind and to the side of the ball, leans back, and drives the instep of the kicking foot through the lower half of the ball with a powerful explosive-like kicking motion. A complete follow-through generates maximum distance (figure 7.7b).

The instep drive is also used to return a ball into play that has traveled over the endline and was last touched by an opposing player. This is commonly called a *goal kick*. The goalkeeper should take goal kicks, as this frees an additional field player to push forward in team attack. The ball is spotted within the goal box and must leave the penalty area before touching another player. The kicker may not touch the ball twice in succession.

Figure 7.7 Instep kick: *(a)* before contact and *(b)* follow-through.

KEY ELEMENTS OF PEAK PERFORMANCE

Instep Kick

1. Approach at a slight angle from behind the ball.
2. Plant the balance foot directly beside the ball for a low serve.
3. Plant the balance foot behind and to the side of the ball for a lofted serve.
4. Square shoulders and hips to target.
5. Position arms out to sides for balance.
6. Keep head steady with vision on ball.
7. Use a powerful snaplike motion of kicking leg.
8. Drive the instep through the center of the ball to serve it along the ground
9. Lean back slightly and drive the instep through the lower half of the ball to serve through the air.
10. Keep the kicking foot extended and firm as it contacts the ball.
11. Use a complete follow-through of the kicking leg.

Distribution Drills

Training to develop better ball distribution should be relaxing and fun for the goalkeeper. The body does not take a pounding, and this is the one aspect of training where the keeper is attacking rather than defending. The exercises on the following pages help keepers improve individual technique. The coach or trainer can assist the keeper in correcting any inconsistencies in execution. Accurate assessment of performance from a knowledgeable coach can lead to productive corrections for the keeper. (For more functional group and team exercises involving goalkeeper distribution, see chapter 11, Initiating Team Attack.)

GOALKEEPER DISTRIBUTION CHART

Type of service	Distance	Advantages
Rolling (bowling)	20 yards or less	Simple technique; high level of accuracy; quick release; easy to control.
Sidearm toss	20 to 30 yards	Ball skims along ground for ease of control; useful for short and medium range distribution.
Baseball throw	20 to 40 yards	Quick release; enables keeper to throw over an opponent blocking the passing lane.
Javelin throw	30 yards or more	Most common method to distribute the ball over distance; throwing motion can be easily altered to change the flight path of the ball.
Full-volley punt	50 yards or more	Direct method of passing most defending opponents by sending the ball into the opposite half of the field.
Half-volley punt (dropkick)	50 yards or more	Lower trajectory generally allows for greater accuracy and ease of control; effective way to quickly change the point of attack.
Instep kick	30 yards or more	Combines the distance of kicking with the accuracy of throwing. Enables keeper to distribute the ball along the ground over greater distances than can be achieved through rolling the ball.

TARGET PRACTICE

Individual Exercise

Equipment   2 to 4 balls, tape, a wall or kickboard

Organization   Use tape to mark several target areas on a wall or kickboard. One target area should be in the upper left corner, one in the right corner, and one in the center. Target areas should be a 3 × 3 yard square, with a 1 × 1 yard square inside the 3 × 3 square.

Procedure   The goalkeeper practices throwing, punting, and dropkicking the ball to targets from various angles and distances. He or she is awarded a point for each time he or she hits the 3 × 3 target and two points when the 1 × 1 target is hit. Play to 10 points and then switch technique.

Training Tips   Choose a specific technique and focus initially on accuracy, then gradually try to increase velocity. Begin at a relatively close distance, 8 to 15 yards, from the center of the goal. After demonstrating proficiency from the center of the goal, move to wider angles and then longer distances.

Variations

1. Work with another keeper and engage in a competition (e.g., first keeper to 10 points wins).
2. Add a server to kick the ball to the keeper. The keeper must collect the serve and then quickly distribute the ball.
3. After the ball is served to the keeper, the server tells the keeper what technique to use so that the keeper must quickly adjust to that technique, as he or she would have to in a game.

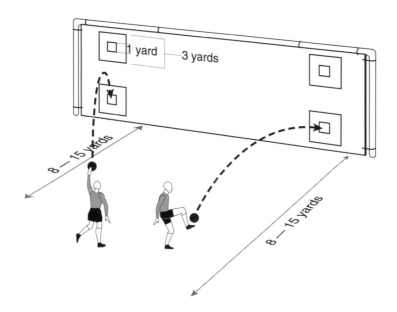

FULL-FIELD TARGET PRACTICE

Individual Exercise

Equipment   2 to 4 balls, cones or disks

Organization   One keeper should be in the goal and another keeper in the intended target area to receive the throw or kick. Use cones or disks to mark target areas at locations throughout the field. Target areas should be strategically placed at various distances, preferably at wide angles. The target areas should be a 5 × 5 yard square, with a 2 × 2 yard square inside the 5 × 5 square. Suggested distances might be as follows:

Target 1—The flank area outside the penalty box
Target 2—The flank area 15 to 25 yards from the penalty box
Target 3—The flank area 20 to 35 yards from the penalty box
Target 4—The flank area 35 yards from the penalty box
Target 5—The areas to each side of the center circle
Target 6—An area 10 to 15 yards beyond midfield

Procedure   One keeper distributes to another keeper who is standing in the target area. For targets 1 to 3, award the keeper one point for each time he or she hits the 5 × 5 target and 2 points for hitting the 2 × 2 target. Increase the point value for targets 4 to 6. Execute 10 repetitions to a target area, total your points, and then switch to another target area.

Training Tips   This exercise can be used after the keeper has picked up the ball with the hands or when the ball must be played with the feet after a back pass. *If using the hands,* the goalkeeper should use the appropriate technique for the intended target and distance. Examples would be as follows:

Target 1—Rolling balls
Target 2—Sidearm throws
Target 3—Baseball throws or javelin throws
Target 4—Javelin throws or dropkicks
Target 5—Javelin throws or dropkicks
Target 6—Dropkicks or punts

Variations

1. The receiving goalkeeper stands 5 to 10 yards from the target area. When the keeper in the goal is ready, the receiver runs to the target area. The keeper with the ball attempts to hit the moving player as he or she arrives in the target area.
2. Place a server outside the penalty area to serve balls to the keeper in the goal. The keeper fields the serve and quickly distributes to the intended target area.

3. Same as number 2 but place the pressure of time on the goalkeeper. Serve balls consecutively for 40 seconds, then total the points.
4. The keeper serves to each target area in a progression, starting with the first target and proceeding to the second, third, and finally to the sixth and final area. Total points and switch keepers.
5. Same as number 4 but use a server to play balls to the keeper.
6. Using the basic procedure and variations, have the goalkeeper distribute with his or her feet after receiving a back pass from the server.
7. Using the same basic procedure, have the keeper take goal kicks and play into the target areas.

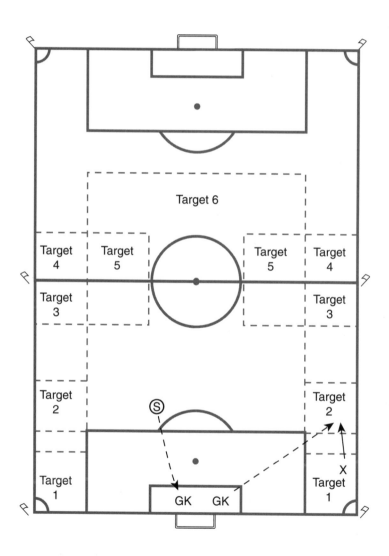

DISTRIBUTION CIRCUIT

Individual Exercise

Equipment   2 to 4 balls

Organization   Four goalkeepers (A, B, C, and D) position at various locations on the playing field. Keeper A is in the goal. Keeper B is in the flank area outside the penalty area. Keeper C is in the center circle, and Keeper D is in the opposite penalty area.

Procedure   Goalkeeper A distributes the ball to Goalkeeper B by rolling it or using a sidearm throw. Goalkeeper B receives the ball and throws it to Goalkeeper C, using a baseball throw. Goalkeeper C receives the ball and

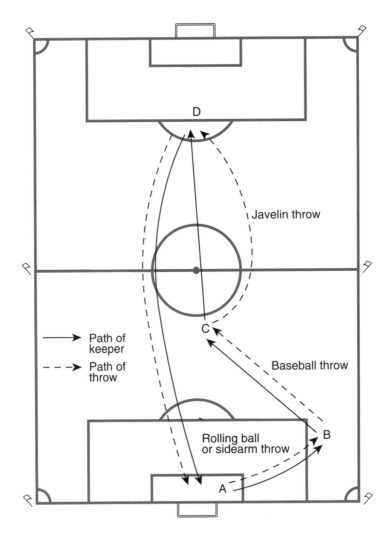

propels it to Goalkeeper D, using a javelin throw. Goalkeeper D then dropkicks or punts the ball back to Goalkeeper A. Repeat the circuit two to five times, then rotate positions. Rotate until each keeper has practiced at each station.

Training Tips   Focus on correct technique; vary the pace and trajectory of each throw or kick.

Variations

1. The distributing goalkeeper should lead the receiving keeper into space.
2. The keepers follow their passes to the next position in the circuit. A fifth keeper or other player is added to receive Keeper D's punt or dropkick.

DROPKICK AND GOAL KICK TECHNIQUE

Individual Exercise

Equipment   6 to 10 balls, 1 regulation goal, cones or disks

Organization   A goalkeeper stands 10 to 15 yards behind the goal with a supply of balls. Set up 3- to 5-yard grids, one outside each corner of the penalty area and one centrally located 10 yards beyond the penalty area. There is a goalkeeper in each grid.

Procedure   The goalkeeper takes a goal kick or dropkicks a ball over the goal to each of the keepers standing in the grids. The keeper serves to a corner grid, then the center grid, and then to the opposite corner. Repeat the circuit two to four times and then switch.

Training Tips   Focus on proper position of the hips and the nonkicking foot to correctly strike the ball to the receiving keeper. Emphasis should initially be on accuracy, striving to hit the receiving keeper inside the grid. Progress this skill by increasing the pace of the dropkick and then by lowering the trajectory.

Variations

1. Instead of going in order, the keepers in the grid signal to each other to communicate who the receiving keeper is. The goalkeeper distributing the ball must constantly reorient body position before dropkicking the ball.
2. Place a server in front of the goal to serve a ball over the goal to the keeper who must field the serve and then dropkick to the appropriate grid.
3. Repeat the same procedure as in variation 1, but have the goalkeeper take goal kicks instead of dropkicks.

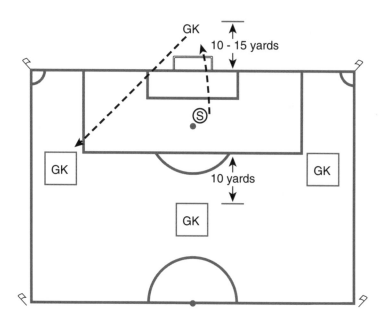

PASSBACK TECHNIQUE

Individual Exercise

Equipment   6 to 10 balls, 1 regulation goal, cones or disks

Organization   A goalkeeper stands 10 to 15 yards behind the goal. A server stands beside the goal with a supply of balls. Set up 3- to 5-yard grids, one outside each corner of the penalty area and one centrally located 10 yards beyond the penalty area. There is a goalkeeper in each grid.

Procedure   The server plays a pass to the goalkeeper, who kicks the ball over the goal to each of the keepers standing in the grids. The keeper should serve to a corner grid, then the center grid, and then to the opposite corner. Repeat the circuit two to four times, then switch.

Training Tips   The keeper focuses on preparing the feet and body as the pass is traveling, so he or she can correctly strike the ball toward the receiving keeper. The emphasis should initially be on accuracy, striving to hit the receiving keeper inside the grid. Begin by striking simple chipped balls, progressing to striking the ball with greater velocity and lower trajectory, especially over longer distances.

Variations

1. Instead of going in order, goalkeepers in the grid signal who the receiving keeper is. The keeper distributing the ball constantly reorients body position before kicking the ball.

2. The server varies the pace and the quality of the back pass, forcing the goalkeeper to adjust to each pass.

3. Move the goalkeeper from behind the goal to the front of the goal. Move the server to the center of the field, 20 to 25 yards from the goal. Move the grids further out, toward midfield, one on each flank and one in the center. You may set up three goals instead. The server plays balls at varied pace and quality to different areas of the penalty area. The keeper kicks these back passes out to the target areas. The keeper should play these balls out first time if possible, using two touches only when necessary.

4. Same as variation 3 but add a player to pressure the keeper during the back pass.

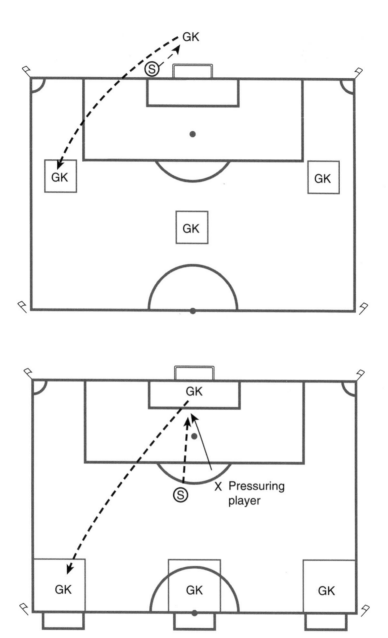

Variations 3 and 4

KEEPER "ASSISTANCE" GAME

Group Exercise

Equipment   2 regulation goals (1 portable), 6 to 8 balls

Organization   Set up a field 40 × 44 yards with goals at each end. Divide the field in half. A keeper should be in each goal, and two other keepers are neutral players on the field. Play 3 v 3 plus the 2 neutral goalkeepers. Balls are placed in each goal and at midfield with the coach.

Procedure   The coach restarts the game when any ball goes over the touchline. The goalkeeper restarts the game with a goal kick after any goal or when the ball goes over the endline. The field players can only score off a throw from the neutral goalkeepers, and it *must* be a first time shot. Any goal off a header or volley is worth two points. The neutral keepers must throw back and forth until they can set up an attacking player. They cannot run with the ball. *When the keeper in the goal makes a save, he or she must pass to one of the neutral keepers in the opposite half to start the attack.* Field players may intercept any pass between the goalkeepers but must play it to a neutral keeper before they can score.

Training Tips   Only the neutral goalkeepers can assist on a goal. All throwing techniques can be used in a fun, gamelike condition.

Variations

1. Allow the keeper in the goal to "assist" on a goal.
2. Allow neutral keepers to score. This forces the defending team to defend more realistically and should open up scoring opportunities.
3. Restrict keepers to using one technique, such as a javelin throw, side-arm throw, and so on.
4. Restrict scoring only to throws that do *not* touch the ground.

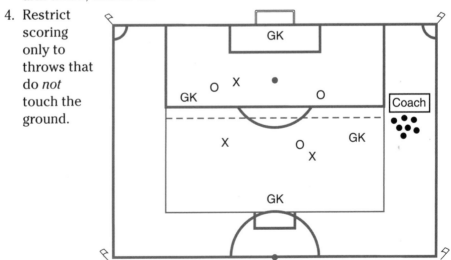

Maximizing Footwork and Range

For our purposes, footwork can be defined as foot movements used to extend all aspects of the goalkeeper's range. The development of proper footwork enhances mobility, extends range, and improves your control of the goal and penalty areas. Correct foot movement can convert a risky, diving save into a routine, standing save. Improved mobility lets you save more shots or, in some cases, even prevent shots from being taken. You become more proficient at cutting off crosses and high balls served into the goal area; in the process, you deny the opposition potential goal-scoring opportunities. By improving your footwork you automatically become a better goalkeeper.

Given its importance, it's surprising that fundamental footwork, such a critical element of goalkeeper performance, is often neglected in training sessions and overlooked when analyzing goalkeeper performance. This is a mistake. Developing fundamental footwork should be a priority. Keepers of all ages and levels, youth and adult, amateur and professional, benefit from footwork training. Goalkeepers and their coaches should constantly strive to improve the keeper's starting position and subsequent foot movements. Small, incremental adjustments in technique can lead to huge improvements in performance.

The basic starting position for all foot movements is the "ready" position (see chapter 3, Receiving Low and Medium-Height Balls). From the ready position, the keeper can quickly shift into any of the eight fundamental foot movements: the side shuffle, collapse step, power step, dropstep, dropstep/crossover step, crossover sprint, backpedal, or vertical jump. Each type of footwork is appropriate for a specific game situation.

Side Shuffle

The keeper uses a side shuffle when moving sideways to position between an oncoming ball and the goal. Proper balance should be maintained with weight centered over the balls of the feet (figure 8.1). Feet should not cross! The primary advantage of shuffling sideways as opposed to turning and running across the goalmouth is that a player can remain in the ready position with shoulders and hips square to the ball. When in the ready position a keeper is able to stop suddenly and set for a shot or quickly reverse direction in response to a sudden change in the flight path of the ball. That said, however, soccer is an unpredictable game. Situations occur during a game when a goalkeeper won't have enough time to shuffle sideways to intercept the flight of the ball. In such cases the best option might well be to turn and run to a spot where the save can be made. When time permits, however, the side shuffle is the preferred foot movement.

Practicing the Side Shuffle. The keeper shuffles sideways from one goalpost to the other along the imaginary "goalkeeper arc" (see chapter 9, Positioning for Maximum Coverage). Begin slowly, then increase speed. As the keeper begins to feel more comfortable with the movement, a coach or teammate tosses balls, and eventually drives shots, at the keeper as he or she shuffles sideways.

Figure 8.1 The side shuffle *(a)* with feet open and *(b)* with feet closed.

Collapse Step

Keepers use the collapse step to receive a rolling ball arriving to their immediate side. In this situation, the keeper needs to get to the ground quickly to make the save. Initiating movement with the foot nearest the ball, he or she steps toward the ball (figure 8.2a), rotates the ankle inward, collapses the leg at the knee (figure 8.2b), and falls to the ground on one side, pinning the ball to the ground with one hand behind and one on top. The lower leg (outside of calf) contacts the ground first, followed by the thigh, hip, and upper body, in that sequence.

Figure 8.2 The collapse step (a) foot movement and (b) on the way to the ground.

Practicing the Collapse Step. The keeper, standing at ready position midway between two balls placed about 10 yards apart, shuffles sideways toward a ball, performs a collapse step, falls sideways to the ground, and pins the ball with both hands. Immediately getting to his or her feet (leaving the ball), the keeper shuffles sideways toward the other ball and repeats the technique. He or she continues shuffling back and forth between balls, each time executing a collapse step before falling and pinning the ball.

Power Step

Mastering the power step improves ability to vault through the air and across the goal. It's the primary foot movement used to initiate the diving save technique. The keeper takes a short sideways step with the foot nearest the ball, flexes slightly at the knee, and pushes off in the direction of the dive (figure 8.3a). Simultaneously, the opposite foot thrusts the opposite leg (farthest from the ball) upward (figure 8.3b). The opposite arm follows to generate additional momentum in the direction of the dive.

Figure 8.3 The power step (a) foot movement and (b) upward movement.

Practicing the Power Step. Standing two yards to the side of a small plastic cone or similar obstacle, the keeper takes a power step toward the cone, flexes at the knee, and vaults over the cone to make an imaginary save. The exercise is repeated from the opposite direction. As the keeper becomes more proficient, a coach or teammate tosses a ball as the keeper vaults over the cone to make the save.

Dropstep

A goalkeeper uses a dropstep when positioning to deal with a ball dropping behind him or her. From the ready position, the keeper takes a step diagonally backward with the foot nearest the ball. For example, if the ball is dropping over the right shoulder, a dropstep is executed with the right foot (figure 8.4). This movement rotates the hips and upper body in preparation to turn the ball over the crossbar and at the same time moves the keeper closer to the goal line. The ball should be kept in sight at all times.

Figure 8.4 The dropstep *(a)* ready position and *(b)* diagonal step backward.

Practicing the Dropstep. The keeper, positioning on the front edge of the penalty area with back to the goal, rotates hips and upper body sideways, dropsteps to the right, and side shuffles once. He or she then squares up and returns to the ready position, rotating body and hips in the opposite direction, dropstepping to the left, and side shuffling once. The sequence is continued (right, left, right, etc.) until the keeper reaches the endline of the field. The head remains steady and buttocks low to the ground. Repeat the exercise several times.

Dropstep/Crossover Step

The dropstep/crossover step is used on those rare occasions when the keeper has been caught well forward off the goal line and must backtrack several steps to handle a ball dropping behind him or her. To perform the movement, a dropstep is executed followed immediately by a crossover step with the opposite foot (figure 8.5). The combined dropstep/crossover step movement enables the keeper to achieve depth and distance in the same movement. The keeper's eyes should remain on the ball as he or she retreats toward the goal line.

Figure 8.5 The dropstep/crossover step: (*a*) dropstep with right foot, and (*b*) crossover of left foot.

Practicing the Dropstep/Crossover Step. The keeper, positioned on the front edge of the penalty area with back to the goal, executes a dropstep right followed by a crossover step with the left foot. He or she then squares hips and shoulders, shifts into the ready position, and repeats the dropstep/crossover step in the opposite direction. The sequence of foot movements continues, alternating right and then left, until reaching the end line. Repeat the exercise several times.

Crossover Sprint

The crossover sprint is an extension of the dropstep/crossover step that is used when the goalkeeper has been caught well off the goal line and the ball has been chipped over his or her head. To perform the crossover sprint, the keeper executes a dropstep/crossover step followed immediately by a sprint toward the goal line (figure 8.6). The keeper angles the head, shoulders, and hips toward the ball as he or she retreats, keeping the ball in sight at all times.

Figure 8.6 The crossover sprint: (*a*) crossover with left foot and (*b*) sprinting with eyes on the ball.

Practicing the Crossover Sprint. Positioned at the left front edge of the penalty area with back to the goal, the keeper executes a dropstep/crossover step to the right followed by a crossover sprint to the right goalpost. The keeper returns to the right front edge of the penalty area and repeats the crossover sprint to the left goalpost. He or she continues practicing the movement for a set number of repetitions.

Backpedal

The backpedal foot movement is used when the keeper is retreating toward the goal line to receive a high lofted ball dropping directly over his or her head. This technique differs from the foot movements mentioned previously in that the hips and shoulders remain square to the ball rather than angled to one side or the other. Use short, choppy steps when backpedaling with weight centered over the balls of the feet. Keep knees slightly flexed with buttocks low to the ground. Lean upper body forward to ensure optimal balance and body control (figure 8.7).

Figure 8.7 The backpedal with (*a*) one leg back, hips low, and (*b*) hands up ready to catch.

The backpedal foot movement is typically observed at the completion of a crossover sprint. It's rarely used as the sole recovery technique but rather as the finishing leg of a recovery run. If the goalkeeper develops proficiency in the dropstep, the dropstep/crossover step, and crossover sprint foot movements, then he or she probably won't need to use the backpedal technique very often.

Practicing the Backpedal. Keeper positions on a touchline (sideline) facing the field and begins a slow jog toward the opposite sideline. Every few yards, he or she executes a 180-degree spin turn and backpedals several steps, then turns again and resumes jogging. He or she continues moving across the field, alternating between the forward jog and backpedal foot movement. The speed of movement should increase as the keeper becomes more comfortable with the backpedal.

Vertical Jump

The foot movements discussed thus far are used to expand coverage of the goal and penalty areas. Mastery of these techniques improves ability to move side to side across the goalmouth, as well as the ability to recover backward to handle a lofted ball dropping near the goal line. It's also important for the keeper to improve range upward, developing the ability to go airborne over teammates and opponents to collect a high ball served into the goalmouth (see chapter 4, Controlling High Balls and Crosses).

In preparation to receive a high ball arriving from the flank, the keeper squares the shoulders and hips to the ball. Judging the flight and moving toward the ball, he or she uses a one-leg takeoff to jump up. Thrust the outside (toward the field) leg upward with knee flexed and pointed toward the ball. Thrust the arms and outside leg skyward in one fluid motion to generate the greatest upward momentum. The inside leg (nearest the goal) remains straight to serve as a stabilizing point upon return to the ground. The jumping technique looks similar to that used when shooting a layup in basketball (figure 8.8).

Practicing the Vertical Jump. Forming a triangle with two teammates (servers 1 and 2), the goalkeeper stands at least 15 yards from the servers. Server 1 begins the exercise by lobbing a high ball toward the keeper, who squares shoulders and hips with the ball and uses a one-leg takeoff to jump up with arms extended overhead. The ball is caught at the highest possible point, brought to the chest, and immediately tossed back to the server. The keeper then returns to the original start position, resets in ready position, and receives a ball tossed by server 2. Continue the exercise for a set number of repetitions, alternating from one server to the other.

Figure 8.8 The vertical jump.

Footwork Drills

Regarding goalkeepers, a common saying among coaches is that "the feet get the hands to the ball." This simple coaching axiom suggests the importance of developing proper footwork. The drills on the following pages break down the foot movements of the goalkeeper while attempting to replicate how they are used in the game. Progress slowly through the following exercises to observe any technical flaws. Once the goalkeeper has demonstrated an adequate level of proficiency in executing the foot movements under minimal pressure, gear up the physical demands by increasing the number or speed of repetitions, or both.

JUMP AND TURN

Individual Exercise

Equipment   10 balls or cones

Organization   Position five balls in a straight line five yards apart. Place an identical line of balls parallel to the first line, about eight yards away. Number the balls 1 through 10.

Procedure   The goalkeeper stands next to ball 1. He or she uses a vertical jump to leap sideways over ball 1, then immediately turns using a dropstep, backpedals to the next ball, turns again, and vertically jumps sideways over ball 2. The keeper continues to ball 5, then shuffles sideways to ball 6, and continues to ball 10. Continue for three to five repetitions of the circuit.

Training Tips   This drill emphasizes the vertical jump, dropstep, backpedal, and shuffle movements. The goalkeeper should never cross legs or turn in a circle when preparing to jump. All vertical jumps should emphasize height, with the knees being driven to the chest.

Variation   Using the same procedure, the goalkeeper should use a forward vertical jump instead of a sideways vertical jump.

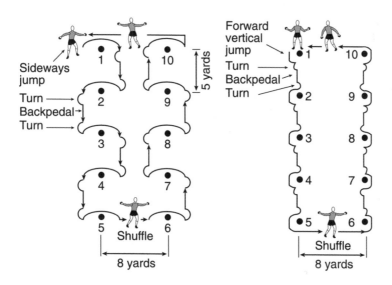

POWER STEP AND FLY

Individual Exercise

Equipment   10 balls or cones

Organization   As in the Jump and Turn, position five balls in a straight line five yards apart. Place an identical line of balls parallel to the first line, about eight yards away. Number the balls 1 through 10.

Procedure   The goalkeeper takes a power step left and jumps over ball 1, then shuffles to ball 2 and again takes a left power step, jumping over ball 2. The keeper continues the same way to ball 5. After jumping over ball 5, the keeper shuffles to ball 6 and repeats the sequence, except now he or she takes a power step with the right foot. Continue for three to five repetitions of the circuit.

Training Tips   This exercise emphasizes the power step and shuffle movements. After each power step, the goalkeeper focuses on having the opposite arm and leg thrust up and over the ball.

Variations

1. The goalkeeper alternates between a left and right power step after each ball. This is accomplished by rotating the hips during the shuffle.
2. Vary the distance between cones, from a minimum of 3 yards to a maximum of 12 yards. This forces the keeper to adjust the shuffling and power step, just as they would in a game.

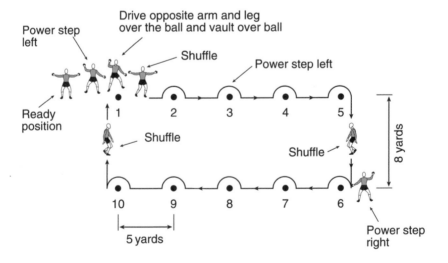

DROPSTEP AND FLY

Individual Exercise

Equipment 8 balls or cones

Organization Place four balls in a straight line eight yards apart. The other four balls are eight yards away, parallel to the first line. Number the balls 1 through 8.

Procedure The goalkeeper stands with back to the first ball. The keeper takes a dropstep right, plants the foot, and leaps over the ball, simulating turning a ball that is dropping over his or her right shoulder. Upon landing, the keeper rotates hips to the left and uses a crossover sprint to the next ball. The keeper then repeats the same sequence, except this time using a dropstep left. Continue the sequence through balls 3 and 4, then backpedal to the opposite line of balls. Repeat the sequence with balls 5 to 8. Continue for three to five repetitions of the circuit.

Training Tips This exercise emphasizes the dropstep, crossover sprint, and backpedal movements. During the dropstep, the goalkeeper focuses on a quick turn with the hips and then thrusts the opposite arm and leg up and over the ball to simulate turning the ball over the crossbar.

Variation Vary the distance between cones from 3 yards to 12 yards. This forces the keeper to adjust the sprinting and the timing of the dropstep, as they would have to do in a game.

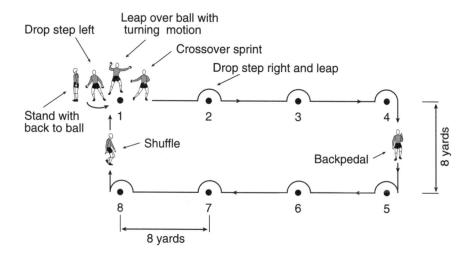

FAST FOOTWORK

Individual Exercise

Equipment 9 balls, cones, or small hurdles

Organization Place nine balls in a straight line a yard apart.

Procedure The goalkeeper stands sideways in the ready position beside the first ball. The keeper steps over the first ball, then the second ball, and continues through the entire circuit of balls, leading with the *left* foot. When stepping over a ball, the lead foot should leave the ground first, followed immediately by the trailing foot. After reaching the last ball, the keeper should quickly backpedal to the first ball and repeat the sequence, except this time leading with the *right* foot. Repeat the exercise six to eight times.

Training Tips The emphasis is on quick feet. The goalkeeper steps over the balls as quickly as possible. Both feet should quickly touch between the balls.

Variations

1. Execute a different foot movement when returning to the first ball.
2. Vary the distance between cones, ranging from one yard to six yards. This forces the keeper to add a shuffle between the balls and to adjust steps over the ball.

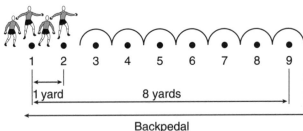

POWER JUMPING

Individual Exercise

Equipment   9 low hurdles or balls

Organization   Place nine hurdles in a straight line a yard apart.

Procedure   Number the hurdles 1 to 9. The goalkeeper executes a vertical jump over hurdle 1 and then immediately jumps backward over hurdle 1. The goalkeeper jumps again over hurdle 1, then over hurdle 2, and back over hurdle 2. Continue the sequence over hurdle 3 through the last hurdle.

Training Tips   This exercise emphasizes the vertical jump. The sequence should always be one jump forward, then one backward, then two jumps forward and one backward. The jump should be as high as possible.

Variations

1. The keeper jumps forward over two hurdles, then once backward, then forward over two hurdles, and then one backward. Continue over all the hurdles.
2. Vary the distance between the hurdles one to two yards.
3. Vertically jump sideways over the hurdles instead of forward.

FAST BACKTRACKING

Individual Exercise

Equipment   10 balls, a regulation goal

Organization   The goalkeeper positions in front of the goal with back to the goal.

Procedure   The goalkeeper is positioned three yards in front of the goal. On command, the keeper takes a dropstep with the left foot, rotating hips and shoulders, and extends the right arm, touching the right hand to the crossbar, simulating turning the ball over the crossbar. Repeat the exercise using the dropstep with the opposite foot. Continue from the same distance with four to six repetitions for each dropstep.

Training Tips   This exercise can be used to practice the dropstep, dropstep/crossover step, crossover sprint, and backpedal.

Variations

1. The goalkeeper stands 6 yards, then 12 yards, and finally 18 yards from the goal. On command, the keeper takes a drop step, followed by a crossover step, then uses a crossover sprint to the goal. The keeper finishes the sprint to goal by simulating turning the ball over the crossbar.
2. Repeat variation 1 except the goalkeeper finishes the sprint by backpedaling the final two to three yards to the goal, simulating catching a high ball.

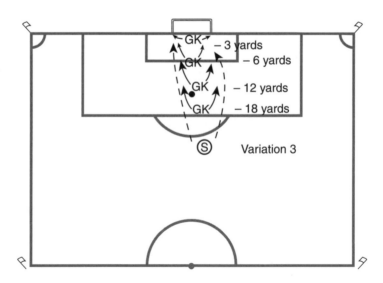

3. Repeat the initial procedure, as well as variations 1 and 2, except now use a server facing the goal. The server should toss balls over the goalkeeper's head near the crossbar as he or she finishes the run, forcing the keeper to turn the ball over the bar or catch it.

Variation 3

COMBINED FOOTWORK

Individual Exercise

Equipment   8 balls or cones and 3 flags

Organization   Organize four balls in a zigzag manner about one to two yards apart. One yard from the fourth ball place three flags in a triangle six yards apart. Place the other four balls in the same manner on the other side of the flags.

Procedure   Shuffle around the balls and flags. Repeat four to six times. (See variations.)

Training Tips   The goalkeeper should adjust foot movements for each ball or flag. He or she should attempt to go through the circuit as quickly as possible, maintaining balance. Jumps should be as high as possible, driving both knees to the chest.

Variations

1. Step over each ball and shuffle around the flags.
2. Vertically jump over each ball and shuffle around the flags.
3. Jump sideways over each ball and shuffle around the flags.
4. Run forward to the first ball, backpedal to the second ball, run forward to the third ball, backpedal to the fourth, and then shuffle around the flags. Repeat the same movements to the balls on the other side.
5. Repeat the initial procedure, as well as variations 1, 2, 3, and 4, except now have a server facing the triangle of flags. The server should strike

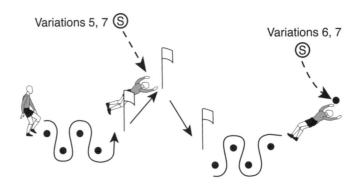

Variations 5, 7 Ⓢ

Variations 6, 7

Ⓢ

ground balls or air balls to the keeper as he or she shuffles between flags.

6. Repeat the initial procedure, as well as variations 1, 2, 3, and 4, but now have a server outside the eighth and final ball. After the keeper finishes his or her final foot movement over the last ball, the server should strike ground balls or air balls to the keeper.

7. Combine variations 5 and 6, but use two servers, one at the flags and one after the last ball.

FORWARD AGILITY AND SAVE

Individual Exercise

Equipment   4 to 6 balls, 3 cones, and 5 flags

Organization   Create a two-yard grid with four flags and put the fifth flag in the center of the grid. Place one cone as a starting point four yards behind the first two flags. Make a goal with two cones, eight yards apart, on the other side of the grid, also four yards from the flags. A server with a supply of balls faces the two cones and the grid at a distance of 8 to 12 yards.

Procedure   The goalkeeper positions at the first starting cone, then quickly sprints around the flags in zigzag fashion. Once the keeper goes around all five flags, he or she goes through the cones to save a shot from the server. Repeat four to six times.

Training Tips   The goalkeeper shifts body weight quickly to get around the flags. Once around all five flags, the keeper sprints forward through the two cones and sets his or her feet to prepare for a shot from the server.

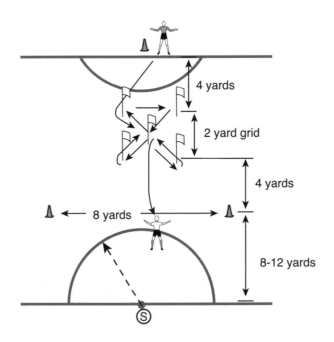

Variations

1. The goalkeeper shuffles to each flag.
2. The keeper must touch the bottom of the flag with his or her closest hand, forcing the keeper to take a step with the foot nearest the flag.
3. The keeper must make two saves in succession after getting to the goal.
4. After sprinting to the first flag from the starting point, backpedal to the remaining four flags, taking a quick dropstep to turn and touch each flag.
5. Use the crossover sprint when going through the flags.

LATERAL AGILITY AND SAVE

Individual Exercise

Equipment   4 to 6 balls, 12 flags or cones, a regulation goal

Organization   Place six flags one to two yards apart in a zigzag manner along the endline. The sixth flag should be set up one yard outside the closest goalpost. The server should be stationed with the balls facing the goal. Place another six flags the same way on the other side of the goal.

Procedure   The goalkeeper sprints around each flag, maintaining good balance. After getting around the sixth flag, the server should hit a shot to the goal. The keeper must prepare his or her feet and make the save. The keeper then begins through the flags on the other side of the goal and makes a save diving to the opposite side. Repeat four to six times.

Training Tips   The goalkeeper should get around the flags as quickly as possible while maintaining a balanced, ready position. Once the keeper is around the sixth flag, he or she gets feet set in a ready position to use the correct footwork (collapse step or power step) for the save.

Variations
1. The goalkeeper shuffles in a ready position to each flag or around each flag.
2. The keeper must touch the bottom of the flag with the closest hand, forcing him or her to take a step with the foot nearest the flag.

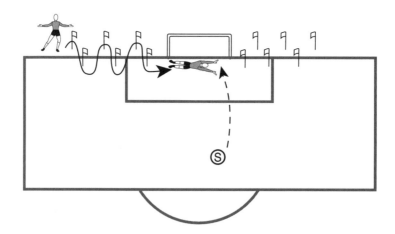

3. The keeper sprints to the first flag and then backpedals to the next flag, alternating forward and backward.
4. Use cones instead of flags so that the keeper can do a vertical jump over the cones.
5. Place six cones in a straight line and have the goalkeeper step over the cones as quickly as possible before making a save in front of the goal.
6. The keeper must make two saves in succession after getting to the goal.

EXTENDING THE RANGE

Group Exercise

Equipment   16 balls, disks, 2 regulation goals (1 portable)

Organization   Create a field 36 × 44 yards. Mark an additional line 4 yards from each goal the width of the goal area. Divide the field in half so there are two penalty areas. There should be eight balls in each goal and eight balls at midfield with the coach.

Procedure   Play 2 v 2 with two neutral players to create a 4 v 2. The goalkeeper's starting position must be outside the four-yard box. The keeper cannot enter that box until the ball is struck. Play would be restarted with the goalkeeper on any ball over the endline or on any goal. The coach restarts the play at midfield when any ball goes over the touchline.

Training Tips   The goalkeeper can control any ball in his or her penalty area. However, the keeper must be prepared to recover quickly to goal to save any ball over his or her head. The focus is on footwork techniques of the dropstep, dropstep/crossover step, backpedal, and crossover sprint.

Variations

1. Extend the keeper's range by making the starting position outside the six-yard box.
2. Add two flank players on each side who play for both teams in a free channel outside the field. Flank players are free to try to shoot on goal. They may also, if the coach desires, enter the field when they receive the ball for a shot from a different angle.

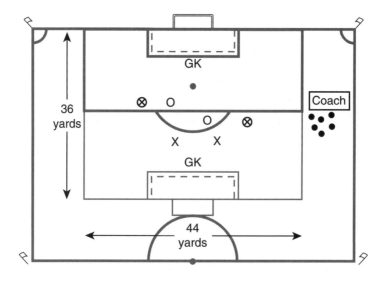

Positioning for Maximum Coverage

When coaches encourage a goalkeeper to "play big," they actually mean to play in a manner that covers the greatest possible area of the goal and penalty areas. Doing so requires the goalkeeper to understand and practice concepts associated with *optimal positioning*. This means that he or she positions to the best possible advantage in relation to the location of the ball and the goal. This rule applies when defending against shots and crosses, as well as when positioning to protect open space behind the last line of defenders. In all cases, the keeper must adjust position in response to the movement of opponents and teammates. Sound positioning is the focal point for every movement performed by the goalkeeper. In most cases, the starting position determines the footwork and technique required to make the save.

The key to optimal positioning is quick and decisive reading of the game. The keeper must read and anticipate, not simply react. The dynamics of the sport are such that the ball and players are constantly moving into different positions on the field. The keeper's adjustment to these movements must be precise. The well-positioned goalkeeper thwarts the opponent's scoring opportunities by stopping shots, saving shots, cutting off crosses, collecting through balls, communicating to teammates, and taking quick, assertive action in every situation. The poorly positioned keeper allows scores. No matter how well executed the dive, if the keeper's angle play is incorrect, he or she may not be able to get to the ball to make the save. Likewise, locating in correct position to field a cross can be the difference between easily controlling the ball and conceding a goal. To consistently maintain proper position requires total concentration, constant analysis, and subtle adjustments. For this reason alone, keepers should be mentally exhausted after a game, even if they weren't physically tested.

The game itself is ultimately the best teacher. There is no substitute for match experience when it comes to improving a keeper's ability to read the game. However, as with many other essential aspects of goalkeeping, developing proper technique through consistent training provides a performance edge. Such training should replicate the game. The keeper will adjust more quickly to situations if he or she has been repeatedly exposed to them during practice sessions. Finally, whether it's during a game or practice, no attack on goal should pass without the goalkeeper closely analyzing his or her position once the play is completed, regardless if the save is made or not. The keeper should learn from every experience.

Positioning for Shots

When positioning to make the save, the keeper needs to consider several factors. The distance of the ball from the goal, the shooting angle avail-

© David Madison/Bruce Coleman Inc.

Good positioning and total concentration on the ball increase a goalkeeper's chances of saving a shot.

able to the player with the ball, the shooting ability of the player on the ball, and the position of opponents in and around the goal area must all be taken into account. In all cases, the goalkeeper must maintain balance and body control while exposing as little of the goal as possible. This is accomplished by playing "off the line"—that is, positioning forward of the goal line. The only instance in which the keeper should position "on the line" is when defending a penalty kick, and this is only because FIFA laws state specifically that the goalkeeper's feet must be positioned on the goal line when the shot is taken. In all other shot-saving situations, the keeper should move forward off the line to narrow the shooting angle.

The Goalkeeper Arc

The "goalkeeper arc" is an imaginary line (arc) connecting the goalposts (figure 9.1) that can assist in positioning to best advantage in relation to the ball and the goal. Anticipate a shot whenever an opponent with the ball is within shooting range of the goal. The keeper aligns his or her body between the ball and the goal by shuffling sideways (see "Side Shuffle" in chapter 8) along the arc. A ball located in the dangerous scoring zone front and center of the penalty area will bring the keeper to a central position along the arc, which narrows the shooter's angle to the goal. As the location of the ball shifts toward the flank, the keeper's movement along the arc brings him or her closer to the near post, enabling him or her to cover a shot directed toward that vulnerable area of the

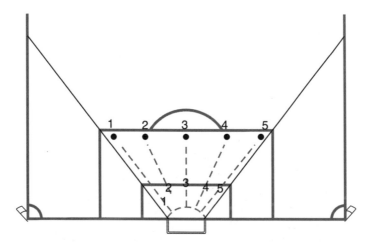

Figure 9.1 As the position of the ball shifts, the keeper must adjust accordingly. The numbers (1 to 5) along the goalkeeper's arc demonstrate the correct goalkeeper positioning in relationship to the changing position of the ball.

goal. As a frame of reference, the keeper should extend the lead arm and hand to feel for the post when nearing it.

The risk of a direct shot on goal decreases when the ball moves near to the endline of the field. In such situations, the keeper anticipates a cross and moves to a more central position along the arc. Proper footwork is essential to maintaining balance and body control. Do not cross legs when shuffling sideways along the arc, as this will limit ability to quickly change direction in reaction to an unexpected or deflected shot.

KEY ELEMENTS OF PEAK PERFORMANCE
Moving Along the Keeper's Arc

1. Assume the ready position in anticipation of a shot.
2. Keep shoulders and hips squared to the ball at all times.
3. Side shuffle along an imaginary line (arc) extending from post to post.
4. Do not cross feet when shuffling sideways.
5. Keep head steady with vision on the ball at all times.
6. Readjust position along the arc to mirror the changing location of the ball.
7. Extend the arm and hand to feel for the near post.
8. If necessary, move forward off the arc to further reduce the shooting angle.

Angle Play

Positioning in relation to the ball and goal is commonly referred to as *angle play*. Experienced keepers play the angles to their advantage. By moving forward off the goal line, they narrow the shooting angle and expose less of the goal to the shooter (figure 9.2). In doing so, they automatically become "bigger" and are able to protect more of the goal area. A keeper becomes better simply by being in the right position at the right time. The following discussion of angle play deals with positioning for shots on goal. A discussion of positioning in relation to a breakaway situation appears in chapter 6, Saving the Breakaway.

One of the most difficult decisions for the keeper is when and how far to advance off the goalkeeper arc. Moving forward too quickly or too far may leave the goalkeeper vulnerable to the chip shot. On the other hand, playing timid and staying back on the line exposes far too much of the goal. Finding a happy balance between the two extremes is the key to success. Moving forward at the proper moment not only narrows the opponent's shooting angle (figures 9.3 and 9.4) but reduces the time the

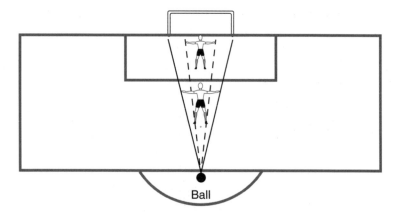

Figure 9.2 An imaginary triangle can be formed with sides extending from the ball to each goalpost. As the goalkeeper moves off the line, advancing toward the ball, the angle is narrowed.

shooter has to look up, see the goal, and pick a spot. Once the keeper has decided to advance off the line, he or she quickly glides ahead in a forward shuffle, with knees flexed. Gliding forward, as opposed to using choppy steps, keeps feet near the ground at all times. This enables the keeper to stop suddenly and set in preparation to make a save. At the moment a shot is released, the keeper's feet should be set and body balanced. In this position, the keeper can react quickly to a low, hard shot or a driven ball in the air.

KEY ELEMENTS OF PEAK PERFORMANCE

Playing the Angles

1. Initiate all movements from the ready position.
2. Use a side-shuffle foot movement to move laterally along the goalkeeper's arc.
3. Glide in a forward shuffle to advance off of the arc to narrow the angle.
4. Keeper shifts into a semi-crouch posture as the distance between keeper and shooter narrows.
5. Maintain balance and body control at all times.
6. Set feet prior to the shot.
7. Always protect the near post.
8. Be prepared to dive in any direction.

Figure 9.3 The goalkeeper ready in the goal.

Figure 9.4 Moving out of the goal to narrow the angle.

Positioning for Crosses

Take into account several important factors when positioning to receive a ball about to be served into the goal area from the flank. These factors include (1) the direction that the ball is rolling (inward toward the goal, outward toward the flank, etc.) as the opponent is about to serve it, (2) the distance between the ball and the goal, (3) the position of the opponent's hips as the ball is served, and (4) the position of players in and around the goal area. A quick analysis of the situation can provide information to enable the keeper to position to best advantage.

In most situations, the keeper's initial position should be at the center of the goalkeeper arc, two or three yards off the goal line. The keeper assumes an open stance with hips square, feet pointed forward (upfield), and upper body rotated in a three-quarter turn toward the ball (see figure 9.5 for correct and incorrect positions). In this posture, the keeper keeps the ball in view and is aware of opponents stationed in and around the goal area.

Protecting the Near Post

Covering the near post area of the goal takes on added significance when an opponent cuts inward from the flank with the ball. The keeper must position to cut off the low cross driven across the goal and, at the same time, be aware that the ball may be cut back to the center of the penalty area or served to the far post. As a general rule, force the opponent to play the most difficult ball, which for most players is the serve to the far post area of the goal. Square up with the ball to pose a "big" (upright) barrier, and move forward to a position even with or a bit beyond the near post. From here, the keeper can cut off the low-driven ball traveling across the front of the goal. He or she also has time to adjust position if the ball is not crossed but instead pulled back to the center of the goal area. Granted, if the ball is lofted or driven to the far post, the keeper will be required to cover a sizeable patch of ground to make the save, but that is also a more difficult ball to play and takes more time to develop.

Reading the Flight of the Ball

The goalkeeper's first priority is to protect the near post area, so he or she should initially position in the front third of the goal. If unsure whether the ball will be crossed to the far post area or driven to the near post, the keeper should readjust to a slightly more central position (but still in the front half of the goal). The position of a player's hips when preparing to serve the ball reveals much about his or her intentions and can help the keeper position to best advantage. When hips are square with the endline

Figure 9.5 Positioning for a cross: *(a)* incorrect position and *(b)* correct position.

and the kicking motion is across the body, the serve will likely be an out-swinger curving away from the goal. In such a situation, the keeper can position more centrally and a bit farther off the goal line. If the opponent's hips are angled toward the goal, then a direct shot on goal or a ball driven across the face of the goal are strong possibilities. An opponent chasing down a ball rolling diagonally away from goal, toward the touchline, usually has to control the ball before crossing it. In this situation, the keeper has a few extra moments to assess the situation and position accordingly, usually by moving toward the back half of the goal and positioning further off the line. An immediate serve may be imminent if an opponent catches up with a ball rolling parallel to the touchline, directly toward the endline. In this case, the location of defending teammates in and around the goal area factors into the keeper's decision on where to position. He or she assesses the situation and obtains answers to these questions. Is a teammate closing down on the ball who can prevent the cross? If so, will that player force the opponent to change direction or hesitate before attempting the cross? Are there teammates positioned to protect the near and far post areas of the goal? Answers to such questions enable the goalkeeper to position to best possible advantage.

Figure 9.6 provides general guidelines for goalkeeper positioning when the ball is located on the flank area of the field. Exact positioning for each situation might vary slightly depending on strengths and weaknesses of the goalkeeper.

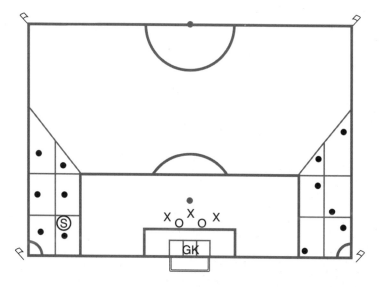

Figure 9.6 Guidelines for goalkeeper positioning when the ball is located on the flank area of the field.

Positioning for Crosses

1. Assume an open stance facing the field.

2. Adjust position and stance according to the angle and distance of the ball from the goal.

3. Be alert for visual cues—position of server's hips, his or her approach to the ball, the angle the ball is traveling.

4. Be aware of defending teammates positioned in and around the goal area.

5. Protect the near post area.

6. Cut off the low-driven ball traveling across the goal.

7. Be confident and aggressive in all actions.

8. Clearly and decisively communicate to teammates.

9. Dominate the six-yard box; control the penalty area.

Linking With the Defense

Controlling the area between the last line of defenders and the goal is one of the keeper's most important responsibilities. The keeper must be prepared to move forward outside of the penalty area to intercept opponent's passes slotted into the vulnerable space behind the defense. In essence, the keeper must assume the role of a "keeper/sweeper," a player responsible for cleaning up anything that filters through the defense (figure 9.7). The following guidelines will assist the goalkeeper in positioning to best advantage. These recommendations should be adjusted to accommodate individual strengths and weaknesses (e.g., footwork, agility, mobility, athleticism, etc.).

- Position near the top of the penalty area when the ball is in the opponent's half of the field and 12 to 18 yards if the ball is in the midfield third but in the opponent's half.

- Withdraw to a position 6 to 12 yards off the goal line when the ball is in the middle third of the field and 12 to 18 yards if the ball is in the midfield third but in the opponent's half.

- Position 3 to 6 yards off the goal line when the ball is located in the defending third of the field but out of shooting range.

There are times when the keeper has to leave the penalty area to play the ball with his or her feet. Choosing the correct moment to move forward to intercept the ball is critical. In most cases, the keeper is punished for even a small miscalculation. A keeper should consider the fac-

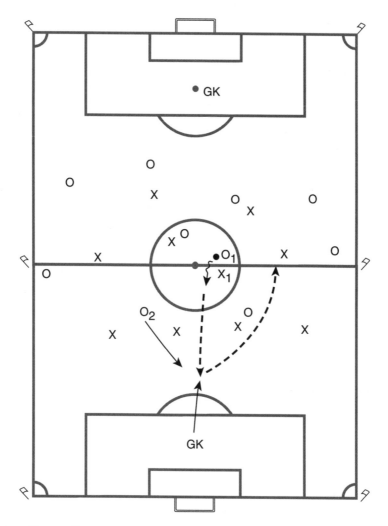

Figure 9.7 The goalkeeper is positioned at approximately the 10-yard line. O_1 with the ball dribbles past X_1 just inside the halfway line and plays a through pass to O_2 making a penetrating run behind the defense. The keeper must leave his or her starting position and play the ball with his or her feet to a teammate.

tors listed below when making the decision if and when to move out of the penalty area:

- Ability to play the ball with the feet. Is the keeper comfortable in that role?
- Speed off the line. Will the keeper be first to the ball?
- Direction and pace of the pass. Is it a dangerous through ball that requires immediate action?
- Position of defending teammates. Is a teammate able to recover and get to the ball before the keeper can?

- Speed and position of opposing players. Can an opponent get to the ball before the keeper can?

Once the decision to go has been made, the keeper must not hesitate. He or she sprints forward to intercept the ball and, if time permits, plays it accurately to a teammate who can initiate a counterattack.

Positioning Drills

A goalkeeper can possess all the athletic ability in the world, but if he or she makes poor decisions about positioning, opponents will take advantage. The aim of the positioning drills that follow is to repeatedly expose the keeper to situations that frequently occur during a match. As the keeper becomes familiar with these situations, he or she will be more able to respond appropriately. In all of these exercises the goalkeeper and the coach or training partner should focus on position rather than technique. Analysis during training eliminates paralysis during the game.

ARC ADJUSTMENTS

Individual Exercise

Equipment 1 regulation goal, 8 to 10 balls

Organization Place 8 to 10 balls in an arc 15 to 18 yards from the goal and inside the penalty area. Use as many players as are available to position behind each ball as servers.

Procedure The players behind each ball go in order around the perimeter. At first they merely take a touch with the ball and prepare their body as if they are shooting. The goalkeeper shuffles along the keeper's arc, aligning with the designated server, maintaining a balanced, ready position, and adjusting to each touch. The goalkeeper completes the arc two to four times.

Training Tips The goalkeeper focuses on proper footwork, a balanced stance, and most important, proper positioning along the keeper's arc.

Variations

1. Increase the speed of repetition; the keeper works with intensity for 60 to 90 seconds.
2. Servers now strike a ball to the goalkeeper. Shots should be served directly to the goalkeeper, so that he or she can concentrate on positioning, not saving.
3. Servers now take an extra touch or two, preferably in a lateral direction, so that the goalkeeper must adjust positioning along the arc.
4. The coach calls out the server who is to take the shot, and the goalkeeper must quickly shuffle in the arc to adjust position and get feet set for a shot.
5. The server passes the ball to another server. The keeper must now shuffle in the keeper's arc while the ball is traveling and get in position before the server takes a shot.

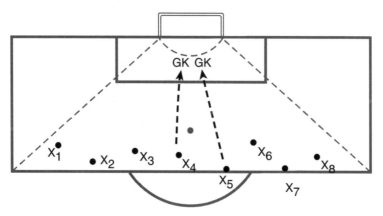

ANGLE ACTION

Individual Exercise

Equipment   1 regulation goal, markers, 8 to 10 balls

Organization   Place 8 to 10 balls in staggered positions, at various angles from the goal, inside the penalty area. Place balls anywhere from 8 to 18 yards from the goal. Place markers in the goal and line it up with the corresponding ball to indicate the goalkeeper's approximate angle and position for that particular ball. If possible, alternate colors of the markers to limit confusion for the keeper. Use as many players as are available to position as servers behind each ball.

Procedure   The players behind each ball shoot in sequential order. The keeper takes a position at the corresponding marker and gets set for a shot. Initially, shots should be directed at the keeper so that he or she can focus solely on correct positioning. The server *does not* take a touch and should hit a dead ball. The keeper stays in the goal until all servers shoot and then switches with another keeper.

Training Tips   The goalkeeper focuses on proper footwork, advancing to narrow the angle, and getting his or her feet set for a shot.

Variations

1. Increase the speed of repetition; the keeper works with intensity for 60 to 90 seconds.

2. Have servers take a touch *toward* the keeper. The keeper's starting angle is still at the corresponding marker, but he or she must now advance beyond the disks when the extra touch is taken. Shots should still be served directly to the goalkeeper so that he or she can focus on positioning, not saving.

3. Have servers take two to three extra touches in a lateral or forward direction so that the keeper must adjust positioning to the ball.

4. The coach calls out the server who is to take the shot, and the goalkeeper must quickly adjust position and get feet set for a shot.

5. The server passes the ball to another server. The keeper quickly moves to the correct angle while the ball is traveling and gets in position before the server takes a shot.

6. As the goalkeeper gains confidence in angles and positioning, the intensity of the shots should be increased, forcing him or her to make difficult saves. Once the intensity of the shots is increased, a 60-second time limit should be placed on the goalkeeper. Shots should be taken rapidly and the markers eventually removed.

GATE GAME

Individual Exercise

Equipment   1 regulation goal, 8 flags or cones, 4 to 8 balls

Organization   Set up four gates marked by flags or cones. The flags are three yards apart. The gates should be set up at the edge of the penalty area: one in each corner of the area and one on each side of the semicircle. A player with a ball is behind each gate.

Procedure   Players dribble through the gates one at a time and take a shot on goal shortly after going through the flags. The goalkeeper takes appropriate starting position and advances to narrow the angle of the shot. Players go in order. The keeper completes the circuit twice and then switches with another keeper.

Training Tips   The keeper focuses on proper footwork, advancing to narrow the angle, and getting feet set for a shot. The goalkeeper is permitted to return to the goal and get a starting position before the next player dribbles through the gate.

Variations
1. Increase the speed of repetition; the keeper works at intensity for 60 to 90 seconds. The keeper is still allowed to get in correct starting position before the next shot is taken, but he or she must immediately get to that position.
2. Players might take an extra touch or two in a lateral or forward direction so that the goalkeeper adjusts positioning to the ball.

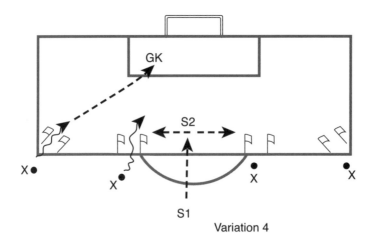

Variation 4

3. The coach calls out the player who is going to go through the gate and take the shot. The keeper quickly adjusts position and gets feet set for a shot.

4. A server passes the ball to another server standing in the box with back to the goal. The server lays the ball off first time toward one of the four gates. The player stationed at that gate sprints through and strikes the ball first time to goal. The keeper now quickly moves to the correct angle while the ball is traveling and gets in position before the server takes a shot.

POSITIONING FOR CROSSES

Group Exercise

Equipment   1 regulation goal, 20 markers, 8 to 12 balls

Organization   Organize four grids between the side of the penalty area and the touchline and two more grids beyond the penalty area but within the flank area. This is done on both sides. If available, place a player in each grid with a ball. If enough servers are not available, place a ball in each grid and have servers move to a different grid after each cross. With markers, divide the goal area into three equal sections, three yards from the goal.

Procedure   Players cross balls into the penalty area from one of the grids, and the keeper adjusts position to the corresponding section of the goal. To minimize the keeper's adjustments, serves should initially come from the grids on one side of the field only. Then serves should switch to the opposite flank after each kick. The keeper fields four to five serves from each flank and then switches with another keeper.

Training Tips   The keeper assumes an open stance when dealing with crosses. The keeper's starting position should adjust according to the angle and distance of the ball from the goal. The keeper uses the markers in the goal to help with positioning. For example, if the server is in a grid close to the penalty area, the goalkeeper may take a position in the front third (near post) section of the goal area. The more confident the goalkeeper becomes in proper footwork, the further his or her starting position should be beyond the goal line, possibly even beyond the three-yard markers and closer to the edge of the goal box.

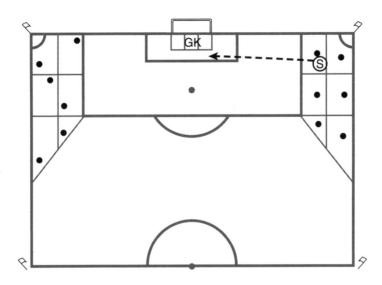

Variations

1. Instead of the servers going in sequential order, the coach indicates which player serves the cross. The keeper immediately adjusts position.

2. The server starts in one grid, and the keeper's starting position corresponds. The server then dribbles into an adjacent grid, and the keeper adjusts accordingly.

3. Add a defender in front of the keeper. The defender varies position and distance from the goal for each serve. The keeper now communicates with the defender.

4. Add attackers and defenders. Play 2 v 1, 3 v 2, or 4 v 3 in the penalty area. Another variable is introduced as the keeper might make positioning adjustments depending on the location of the defenders and attackers.

STAYING CONNECTED

Team Exercise

Equipment   2 regulation goals, 10 markers, 4 to 6 balls

Organization   Divide the field into thirds using markers. Organize a line of three or four defenders (depending on how many defenders are used by your team). Set up another team of eight attacking players, including three in the back third of the field, three in the middle third, and two in the attack third.

Procedure   The attacking team plays hand ball, moving the ball quickly by throwing and catching. The defending team cannot intercept the pass, focusing solely on positioning. Three attacking players are allowed only in the back third of the field, and three attacking players remain in the middle third. The two forward players can move into the attack or midfield third. Defenders move vertically and horizontally, depending on position of the ball. Offside is in effect.

Training Tips   The goalkeeper stays connected by moving vertically and laterally with the defenders. He or she moves up and back with the defenders, never staying in one position, especially when in the goal. Here are some suggestions:

1. *Defending third.* If the ball is in the far third of the field (the attacking team's defending third of the field), the keeper moves out to the edge of the penalty area or slightly beyond to the top of the semicircle. The keeper then commands the defenders to move up close to midfield.

2. *Midfield third.* If the ball is in the midfield third of the field but in the defensive half, the keeper should be 6 to 12 yards from the goal. If the ball is in the midfield third of the field but in the opponent's half or beyond, the keeper should be 12 to 18 yards from the goal. The defenders should move up close to the midfield line.

3. *Attack third.* If the ball is played into the attack third, the keeper should be 3 to 6 yards from the goal, with defenders taking a position at least at the edge of the penalty area.

4. Once the ball is in shooting range (15 to 20 yards), the keeper should position in the goalkeeper's arc.

The keeper communicates to the defenders when to step up, when to recover, and when to tuck in from the weak side. Staying connected allows the goalkeeper to communicate to the defenders and be close enough to read any through passes. How far the keeper's starting position is from the goal depends on the ability of the keeper to recover to the goal to avoid being "chipped."

Variations

1. Permit the attacking team to use their feet. Attackers still play simple possession, and defenders cannot intercept the ball, still focused primarily on moving up and back as a unit attached to their keeper.

2. So that the keeper maintains a realistic starting position, permit the attacking team to play through balls and to attempt chip balls over the keeper's head.

3. Add three to four defending midfielders in front of the defenders. The midfield line, the back line, and the goalkeeper stay connected and move together.

4. Gradually add attacking and defending players until there's an 11 v 11 game.

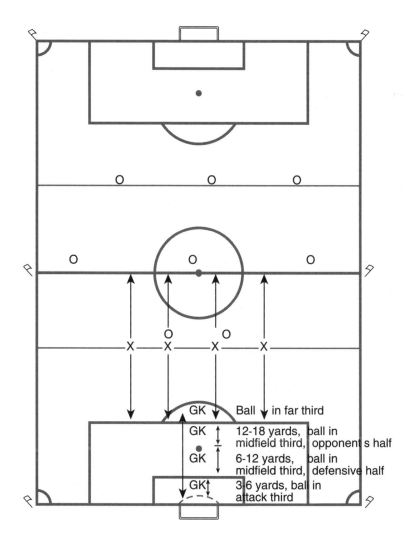

Defending Restart Situations

Restarts include direct and indirect free kicks, corner kicks, throw-ins, and penalty kicks. Commonly called "dead ball" or "set piece" situations, restarts pose a special challenge for the goalkeeper because they provide opponents an opportunity to execute a rehearsed play. A significant percentage of goals scored at higher levels of competition come on dead ball situations. For instance, more than 30 percent of the goals scored in World Cup 1998 came off restarts. In the World Cup final, France scored two of its three goals off set pieces to win the world title. It's clear that a team's ability to successfully defend in restart situations can be the difference between winning and losing. Defensive organization in these situations is essential to team success and should be practiced and rehearsed during training sessions. Every player on the team, including the goalkeeper, should understand and accept his or her role in the process.

Corner Kicks

Corner kicks can be grouped into three general categories. The near-post corner is designed to attack the space on the side of the goal nearest the ball. The ball is driven low and hard toward the near corner of the six-yard box. One or more attacking players simultaneously make runs into that area to intercept the ball and direct it on goal. The *far-post corner* is designed to exploit the space near the goalpost farthest from the ball. The ball is served toward the far side of the goal, generally 8 to 12 yards out from the endline. Preplanned runs by the attacking players are used to draw defenders into poor positions and create space for a strike on goal. The *short corner* provides a third option. Rather than serve the ball directly into the goalmouth, the kicker touches the ball to a teammate positioned nearby who attempts to penetrate the defense by dribbling or by swerving the ball into the goal area.

Position of the Goalkeeper

The keeper's positioning depends on the type of service (in-swinger or out-swinger), the ability of teammates to challenge for air balls served into the goal area, and his or her ability to handle crossed balls. For most corner kicks, the keeper positions in the center or front third of the goal (nearest the ball), one or two yards off the goal line, assuming an open stance facing upfield with upper body and head rotated toward the ball (figure 10.1). In this posture the keeper can keep the ball in sight and be aware of opponents entering the goal area from the backside. The keeper should not square up and face the corner of the field where the ball is spotted. From that position, view of the penalty area is restricted, and it's difficult to handle a ball flighted to the far post area.

Figure 10.1 In an open stance for a corner kick.

Position of Field Players

Even the best goalkeepers can't cover the entire goal area. Positioning teammates to protect the most vital space makes the keeper's job easier. There are five critical areas in the goal area where defending players should position (see figure 10.2).

- Area 1. Position one player 12 to 15 yards from the kicker to prevent a low driven ball into the near post area. If you've scouted the opponents and know they may attempt a short corner, it's advantageous to have two players front the ball.
- Area 2. Position one teammate inside the near goal post. This player is responsible for blocking any shot or deflection to the near post corner of the goal.
- Area 3. Position one teammate even with the near post on the edge of the six-yard box. This player is responsible for cutting off a ball driven into that area.
- Area 4. Position one or more players to protect the far post area of the goalmouth. Remaining field players can either man-mark opponents in the goal area or position in zonal coverage to protect specific areas of the goalmouth. In either case all defending players should position goal side and ball side (between the ball and the opponent they are marking) at the moment the kick is taken. Defenders must be in position to beat their opponent to the ball.
- Area 5. Position one or more players between the penalty spot and edge of penalty area to clear away any knockdowns.

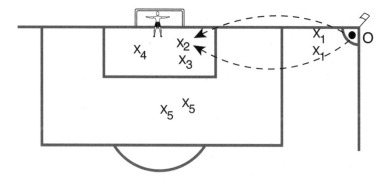

Figure 10.2 When defending a corner kick, the field players are positioned to protect the five critical areas of the goalmouth.

Throw-Ins

Although the primary function of a throw-in is to return the ball into play after it has crossed over a touchline, in certain situations the throw-in is used as a scoring weapon as well. Most high school, college, and professional teams have one or more players who can toss the ball with accuracy and velocity over distances of 30 yards or more. Thus, when opponents are awarded a throw-in within the defending third of the field, the goalkeeper must be prepared to defend the long throw-in.

In terms of organization, the long throw-in can be considered a variation of a corner kick and be defended in a similar manner. The primary difference is the angle at which the ball approaches the goal. Corner kicks are always taken from the endline, with the ball spotted in the half-arc at the corner of the field. A throw-in may be taken from anywhere along the sideline, depending on the spot where the ball left the playing field. In either case the goalkeeper should dominate the goal box and be the first player to the ball as it enters the goal area. He or she should catch the ball, if possible—if in doubt, box it out of the danger area.

Free Kicks

As the name implies, a direct free kick is one from which a goal can be scored directly from the kick against the offending team. An indirect free kick is one from which a goal cannot be scored unless the ball has been touched by a player other than the kicker before passing through the goal. The nature of the rule infraction determines the type of free kick. Indirect free kicks are signaled by the referee holding one arm above his or her head. There is no referee signal to indicate a direct free kick.

Common fouls penalized by awarding a direct free kick include

- kicking or attempting to kick an opponent,
- striking or attempting to strike an opponent,
- tripping or attempting to trip an opponent,
- pushing or holding an opponent,
- intentional handling of the ball by a field player,
- handling of the ball by the goalkeeper outside of the penalty area, and
- making a violent charge.

Common fouls penalized by awarding an indirect free kick include

- being offside,
- obstructing an opponent,

- taking more than six seconds for the keeper to release the ball,
- playing dangerously, and
- exhibiting unsportsmanlike behavior.

Direct and indirect free kicks spotted outside the penalty area but within shooting range of the goal pose a legitimate scoring threat. All defending players must position at least 10 yards from the ball until it has been kicked. The goalkeeper's top priority here is to position with a clear view of the ball. At the same time, several teammates should position side by side 10 yards from the ball, forming a wall between the ball and the goal. It is the keeper's responsibility to communicate how many players should position in the wall. As few as two and as many as five defenders can make up the wall, depending on the location of the ball, its distance from the goal, and the ability of the kicker. For example, a free kick spotted front and center of the goal just outside of the penalty area requires more players in the wall than a free kick spotted on the flank, where the shooting angle to the goal is much narrower (figure 10.3). Players not included in the wall usually mark opponents positioned in the vicinity of the goal or, if the team is organized zonally, position to protect the most critical spaces in and around the goal.

When the referee has signaled an infraction against the defending team within scoring range of the goal, it's imperative that the wall be formed quickly and positioned properly. This requires planning and prematch preparation. Most teams designate a field player to "post" the wall. After the referee spots the ball the post player immediately positions 10 yards from the ball along an imaginary line connecting the near goal post and

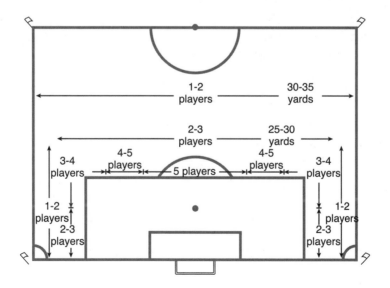

Figure 10.3 General guidelines for forming a wall.

the ball (figure 10.4). Teammates line up side by side *to the inside* of the post player. The wall of players is positioned to block a shot directed at the near-post half of the goal. The goalkeeper is generally responsible for protecting the far-post half of the goal.

An indirect free kick spotted *within* the defending team's penalty area poses a real challenge for the goalkeeper. In this situation, the keeper may decide to position additional players in the wall, depending on the location of the ball and its distance from the goal. The keeper usually positions behind the wall and in line with the ball, except for the special situation where the ball has been spotted within 10 yards of the goal. In such a case, the wall of players positions on the goal line, and the goalkeeper positions in the middle of the wall in direct line with the ball.

Figure 10.4 The goalkeeper should line up the post player. The keeper then calls out the number of players in the wall and those players should immediately line up inside the post player. A field player may make any final adjustments, but ultimately this is the keeper's responsibility.

Penalty Kicks

The penalty kick provides the ultimate one-on-one test for the keeper. Awarded for a direct foul committed by the defending team within its own penalty area, the ball is spotted 12 yards front and center of the goal. Only the designated kicker and the goalkeeper are permitted to position within the penalty area and penalty arc until the ball has been kicked. Federation International de Football Association (FIFA) Law 14 states that the goalkeeper must position with feet on the goal line. The keeper is permitted to move laterally along the line prior to the kick but may not move forward off the goal line until the ball has been played. Wild antics by the goalkeeper designed to unnerve the kicker, such as shouting or waving the arms, are considered unsportsmanlike and are prohibited.

There's no consensus among goalkeepers on the best method for defending a penalty kick. Correctly anticipating which way the shooter will go is half the battle. Some keepers prefer to use prekick movement along the goal line to distract and unsettle the kicker. Others prefer to focus on subtle cues that may reveal the kicker's intentions, such as the position of the player's hips when approaching the ball. Some keepers simply pick one side of the goal and dive in that direction in hope that the kicker has chosen to shoot to that side. Through practice and experience, each keeper adopts (and adapts) a method that works best for him or her.

In preparation to make the save, the goalkeeper assumes a posture similar to the basic ready position, with feet on the goal line. He or she leans slightly forward with weight evenly distributed and centered over the balls of the feet. As the kick is taken, the keeper vaults sideways parallel to or slightly forward of the goal line to narrow the shooting angle. If the keeper gets hands to the ball but can't hold it, he or she should try to box it or deflect it wide of the goal. Rebounds in front of the goal should be avoided, as the kicker is permitted to move forward after taking the penalty kick to finish a ball that rebounds off the keeper.

To improve chances of saving a penalty shot, the keeper is alert to subtle cues inadvertently provided by the kicker just before and during the approach to the ball. Picking up on bits of information might help in calculating the shooter's intentions.

Before the kick

- Watch the kicker's eyes and mannerisms. The eyes might glance toward one side of the goal, revealing where the kicker intends to drive the ball. Of course, a sly opponent might purposely look toward one area of the goal to try to throw the keeper off. The more experienced keepers become in observing, the more they learn what to watch for, and the less they must rely on guesswork.

© EMPICS Sports Photo Agency/Adam Davy

Bayern Munich's Stefan Effenberg takes a penalty kick.

During the approach to the ball (based on a right-footed kicker)

- Angle of approach. A kicker who approaches the ball at a sharp angle most likely aims the shot to the goalkeeper's left. From an angled approach, it's difficult for the kicker to pull the ball back toward the right corner of the goal. A kicker who approaches the ball from directly behind is more likely to shoot the ball to the goalkeeper's right, or possibly straight down the middle, anticipating that the goalkeeper will move.

- Position of the kicking foot. When the kicking foot is positioned sideways-on, the shooter will most likely attempt to push the ball to the goalkeeper's left. If the kicking foot is extended down and pointed inward, the kicker will probably strike the ball with the full instep and attempt to drive it to the goalkeeper's right.

- Position of shoulders and hips. Body position can be a very revealing clue. In most cases, the shooter's hips and shoulders will square with the intended target (area of the goal) at the moment the ball is contacted. In such situations, the keeper must make a last-second decision and adjust as necessary.

Making the big save on a penalty kick can change the complexion of the game and determine the outcome. A combination of factors—anticipation, athleticism, technique, and sometimes just plain old luck—determine a goalkeeper's degree of success on penalty kicks. As is true of virtually all goalkeeper skills, the ability to save penalty kicks can be improved through repetitive practice. Thus, it's important to devote adequate practice time to perfecting technique.

Restart Drills

The most effective individual and group exercises involve the goalkeeper simply saving free kicks, penalties, and corner kicks. The more repetitions, the better. It's also important for the keeper to practice many different serves to become comfortable in virtually any situation. Make practice situations realistic. Use a wall when training to save free kicks so the keeper becomes accustomed to positioning with a limited view of the ball. Portable kickwalls are available if you're willing to spend the money; if not, teammates can help by volunteering to form a wall. When practicing to defend corner kicks, the keeper should face both in-swinging and out-swinging corners to simulate situations faced in games. The same holds true when training to save penalty kicks. Attempt many different types of kicks so that the keeper learns to make quicker adjustments during games. Defending the long throw-in is another area that requires individual practice. The rotation and approach of the ball is very different from that of a corner kick, so keepers should practice defending both.

The key to defending restarts is team organization, within which the goalkeeper is the focal point. The following exercises involve the entire team. Because restarts are one of the few instances during a game where situations can be rehearsed, it's crucial that the goalkeeper and field players be on the same page. Note that both of the following exercises end in a controlled 11 v 11 situation. The best way to rehearse gamelike situations is to play the game.

DEFENDING CORNER KICKS

Team Exercise

Equipment 1 regulation goal, 4 to 6 balls

Organization Organize a half-field practice, starting with at least eight attackers and four defenders. Have one defender zone the near post area and another the central part of the goal. A third player should be on the near post and one other player on either the far post or zoning the far post area. The attacking team should have one player taking the corner kick, three to four players making runs to the goal, and three to four in specific areas in the box.

Procedure The attacking team serves corner kicks into the goal area, while the defending team attempts to win the ball and clear it out of the penalty area.

Training Tips Practice in-swinging and out-swinging serves for corner kicks along with the proper timing of runs for effective, dangerous attacking corner kicks. Runs should be to the key areas: near post, far post, and central part of the goal.

   The goalkeeper positions the defenders first and then gets set in the front half of the goal in an open stance, two to four yards off the goal line. The keeper adjusts position in anticipation of an in-swinging or out-swinging corner kick.

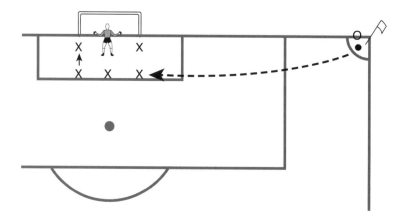

Variations

1. Play 9 v 6 and allow for two extra defenders to pick up runners into the goal area. The goalkeeper should let defenders know who the most dangerous runners are.

2. Play 11 v 8 + 2 to increase the number of defenders marking attackers. Once the ball is cleared, the goalkeeper commands the defenders to get out of the penalty area. Defenders then sprint out of the area. If defenders or the keeper win the ball, they should immediately distribute to one of the 2 players located on each flank near midfield.

3. Play 11 v 11, full pressure, in a controlled half-field scrimmage.

DEFENDING SET PIECES

Team Exercise

Equipment   1 regulation goal, 4 to 6 balls

Organization   Organize a half-field 11 v 11 practice. The attacking team should have two to three players taking free kicks and three to four players making runs to the goal.

Procedure   The attacking team takes free kicks from various distances and angles, the coach dictating where the kicks are taken. The keeper organizes the wall and positions remaining defenders, then assumes a correct starting position. The defending team attempts to win the ball and clear it out of the penalty area. The attacking team runs five to six plays in rapid succession from different areas, so the keeper and defenders need to get quickly organized.

Training Tips   The goalkeeper calls out the number of players in the wall. The keeper, before getting in correct starting position, then positions a defender to guard the near post. The keeper adjusts position in anticipation of the angle and distance of the kick and also makes sure defenders are organized away from the ball.

Variations

1. Once the ball is cleared, the keeper commands defenders to get out of the penalty area. Defenders sprint out of the area. If defenders or the goalkeeper win the ball, they immediately distribute it to one of two players located on each flank near midfield.
2. Play 11 v 11, full field, in a controlled scrimmage. The coach should blow the whistle frequently at various spots on the field so that restarts are rehearsed from realistic positions.

Initiating
Team Attack

The defending third of the field nearest to your goal is considered the zone of "no risk," an area where possession of the ball is of paramount importance. A poor pass or bad decision in the defending third might well result in a goal scored. Thus, a team needs to develop a strategy for advancing the ball safely and effectively out of the back third of the field. Methods used to initiate team attack will differ from one team to the next depending on the ability of the players and the philosophy of the coaching staff. What works well for one team might not work for another. Highly skilled teams often choose to advance the ball methodically through short possession-oriented passing combinations, but this would not be appropriate for a team whose players possess limited technical ability, as they would be more likely to make an errant pass in a critical area of the field. A team whose players possess a high degree of athleticism might attempt to maximize that strength by employing a quick strike offense. Rather than use short passing combinations to methodically work the ball out of the back, they instead send it directly into the opponent's half of the field through long direct passes, either from the goalkeeper or the back line of defenders. Methods used to initiate team attack may also vary from one game to the next depending on weather conditions, field surface, and opponent's style of play. There's no right way or wrong way to advance the ball—the method that works best for a team should be the method of choice. In what follows we'll examine common strategies used to advance the ball into the middle and attacking thirds of the field once the goalkeeper has gained possession of the ball.

Combination Play Through the Defending Third

The emphasis here is on maintaining possession of the ball while advancing through the middle and into the attacking third of the field. The goalkeeper usually distributes the ball to a teammate by rolling it, or possibly via a sidearm toss (see chapter 7, Distributing the Ball). The primary advantage of using short- and medium-range passing combinations to advance the ball out of the back is that the team is able to move forward as one compact unit (figure 11.1). This strategy is most effective against teams that do not press forward and employ high-pressure tactics in your de-

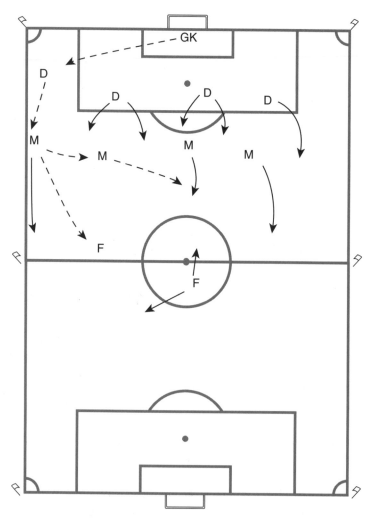

Figure 11.1 Combination play through the defending third—possible options.

fending third, which allows your players time and space to move the ball forward. It does have limitations, however. Because the build-up is somewhat methodical and the ball advanced rather slowly, defending players have ample time to consolidate goalside of the ball.

To successfully build out of the back, a team must create passing lanes through which the ball can be played forward. This is accomplished by the back line of defenders spreading across the field from one touchline to the other once the ball is in the goalkeeper's hands. The keeper initiates play by distributing the ball to a defender. Passing lanes are created by drawing opponents to the area of the ball and then switching the point of attack (location of the ball) to exploit open space away from the ball. Sound decision-making, confidence with the ball, and an ability to serve the ball accurately over distance are required for this strategy to work effectively.

Playing Directly Into the Middle Third

To use this strategy effectively, the goalkeeper must be able to throw the ball accurately over distances of 30 yards or more. After gaining control of the ball, the keeper runs forward to the top of the penalty area and releases the ball directly to a midfielder—or possibly to a striker checking back into the middle third of the field. If the passing lane to the target is open, use the sidearm-throw technique to skim the ball along the ground to a teammate's feet. If the lane is blocked, use the baseball- or javelin-throw technique to lob the ball over the top. By throwing the ball directly into the middle third of the field, you effectively eliminate the possibility of possession loss in your end of the field (figure 11.2).

Playing Directly Into the Attacking Third

The safest and surest way to avoid loss of possession in your half of the field is to throw or kick the ball directly into the opponent's end. The primary advantage of playing directly into the attacking third (figure 11.3) is that the ball is immediately placed behind a majority of opponents. This strategy can be used effectively to counter a team that attempts to press (apply high-pressure tactics) in your end. It's also a good choice during the waning moments of a game, when a team is protecting a lead and doesn't want to risk possession loss in their end.

The three primary techniques used by the goalkeeper to play the ball directly into the attacking third are the javelin throw, the full-volley punt, and the dropkick (see chapter 7, Distributing the Ball). The javelin throw is probably the most accurate of the three methods, although some keepers can send the ball just about where they want to using the dropkick. In

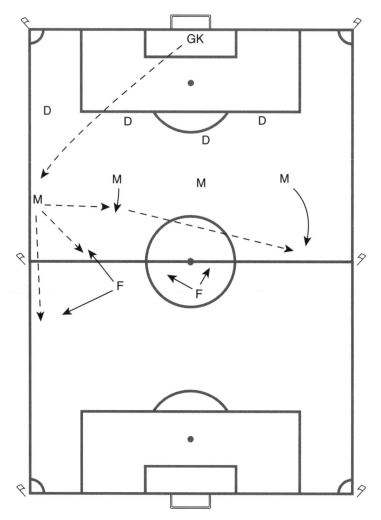

Figure 11.2 Playing direct into the middle third—possible options.

both cases, the ball has a lower trajectory than the full-volley punt and is generally easier to receive and control. On the flip side, the goalkeeper can probably generate greater distance with a full-volley punt than with a javelin throw or dropkick.

Which Strategy Is Best?

Which strategy works best depends on game situation and strengths and weaknesses of players comprising the team. No single method of initiating team attack is inherently better or worse than another. What fits well with one team might not fit another. What works successfully against one opponent may not work against another. Approach each game and each

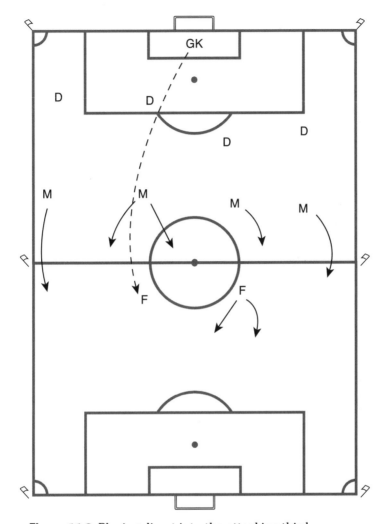

Figure 11.3 Playing direct into the attacking third.

opponent differently, and change strategy accordingly. Regardless of the method employed to initiate the attack, the goalkeeper is ultimately responsible for establishing the rhythm and setting the tone. He or she must be decisive and confident in physical actions and verbal commands. Throws, punts, and dropkicks must be timely and accurate. After distributing the ball, the keeper can help coordinate the action by communicating to teammates.

Initiating Team Attack Drills

The group and team exercises provided here revolve around team play. The goalkeeper's primary responsibility is to get the process started effectively and then support the play. Teammates do their part by performing their designated roles. Effective communication, organized movement, and proper positioning of all players make the goalkeeper's job considerably easier. The exercises that follow focus on specific situations designed to enhance decision-making and improve execution through rehearsing scenarios a goalkeeper will likely encounter on game day. (Note that exercises designed for developing individual ball distribution skills are in chapter 7, Distributing the Ball.)

THREE-GOAL PASSBACK GAME

Group Exercise

Equipment   4 to 6 balls, 2 regulation goals (1 of them portable), 2 portable small-sided goals or flags

Organization   Set up the portable regulation goal at midfield in the center circle. Set up the small-sided goals at the flank areas of midfield. The coach is about 20 to 30 yards from the goal, outside the playing area, with a supply of balls to start and restart the exercise.

Procedure   Play six attackers versus four defenders. The six attackers get two points for every goal scored. The defenders get one point by scoring on the flank goals at midfield. They get two points for any ball the goalkeeper plays into one of the three goals at midfield after a passback. The offside law must be observed. As rules state, any ball over the endline by the attacking team should be restarted as a goal kick. The goalkeeper should also take all goal kicks to simulate game conditions. Keepers receive one point for any goal scored from a goal kick.

Training Tips   Defenders should look to maintain possession by having the confidence to play the ball to the goalkeeper's feet. The goalkeeper should always seek to initiate the attack by passing the ball to a target, preferably a wide player. When attempting passbacks, the keeper and the defender need to have verbal and/or visual communication. The keeper needs to let the defender know where and to which foot he or she wants the ball passed. The defender needs to convey that he or she is prepared to play the ball back.

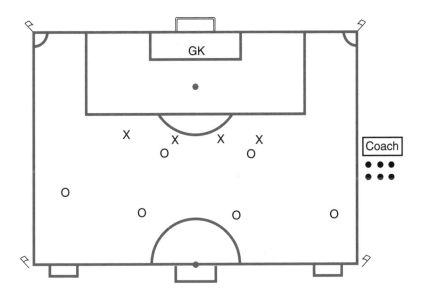

Variations

1. Vary the point system. For example, award three points if the keeper plays the ball into a flank goal and only one point if the ball is played into the central goal.

2. If four small-sided goals are available, play 4 v 4 plus two neutral players in the half-field. This option allows two goalkeepers to be involved in essentially the same exercise. The keepers defend the regulation goals and attempt to play any back passes to the small-sided goals on the flank. The point totals remain the same.

SWITCHING THE POINT OF ATTACK

Group Exercise

Equipment   6 to 8 balls, 1 regulation goal

Organization   Organize four flank players, one on each flank between the penalty area and the touchline and one on each flank near midfield. A server or the coach should be in the center circle near midfield.

Procedure   The coach plays a ball to the flank player nearest the corner. This player crosses a ball to the goalkeeper. The keeper catches the cross and immediately switches the point of attack by distributing to the opposite flank player. This player pushes the ball upfield to the flank player on his or her side of the field, who then returns the ball to the coach in the center. The coach then continues the play by serving to either flank player in one of the corners, and the exercise is repeated. Do 10 to 20 repetitions.

Training Tips   The goalkeeper should be thinking to switch the play as soon as the cross is caught. Field players should be thinking to open up to receive a throw from the keeper as soon as the cross is taken from the opposite flank.

Variations

1. Add a wide defender between the flank players. The defender must mark one of the flank players, and the goalkeeper must distribute to the open player.
2. Add two players at midfield, one on each side of the center circle. The goalkeeper now has the additional option of playing to the player at midfield. The defenders must allow the cross to be played.
3. Add two more defenders at midfield. These defenders can mark either one of the flank players or one of the players at midfield, increasing the keeper's decision-making. The defenders must allow the cross to be played.
4. Add a permanent central defender. The four players, who have been defending once the keeper distributes the ball, are now allowed to go to goal and attack the crosses. The crosses now become live balls. However, once the keeper gets possession, they must drop off to defend the keeper's outlet pass and deny the ball to be played to the coach. Once the coach has possession, the play is restarted with a pass to a flank player for a cross to the goalkeeper.

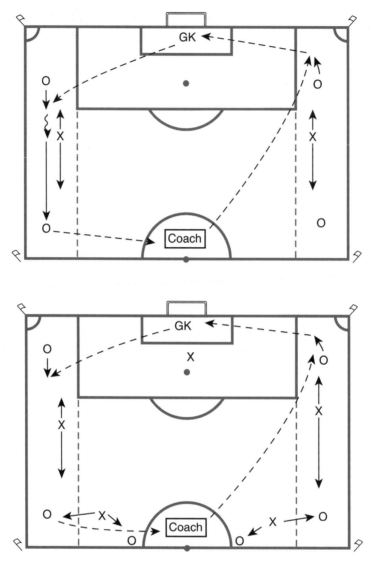

Variation 4

BUILD-UP GAME

Group Exercise

Equipment   2 portable regulation goals, disks, 6 to 8 balls

Organization   Place goals on the edge of the penalty areas to serve as the endline. Mark a channel several yards in from the touchline. Play 7 v 7 with four free, neutral flank players. A flank player is stationed inside the channels in each half of the field. Preferably, players are organized into a 2-3-2 system.

Procedure   Play regular 7 v 7, using the unchallenged flank players to build out of the back by maintaining ball possession and ensure accurate crosses. The goalkeepers, however, are restricted to distributing *only* to the flank players. If the keeper distributes to the flank player in his or her half of the field, that player must look to continue the play only in the same half of the field to ensure a more methodical build-up. If the goalkeeper distributes to the flank player in the attacking half of the field, the attacking team may go directly to goal. Regular soccer rules apply, so any ball sent over the endline by the attacking team should be restarted as a goal kick. To simulate game conditions, the goalkeeper should also take all goal kicks.

Training Tips   The goalkeepers must decide whether to slow the game down by playing to a flank player in the defending half of the field or speed up the game by playing directly into the attacking half of the field. The emphasis should be on using a throwing technique to distribute to the flank players. The passback rule applies, and goalkeepers should seek to distribute any back passes to the flank players also. Keepers also should attempt to switch the point of attack after making a save.

Variations

1. Flank players in the defending half of the field are allowed to play a ball to the strikers in the attacking half of the field.
2. Goalkeepers are permitted to distribute with a throw or kick to the strikers in the attacking half of the field.
3. One flank player from each half of the field can enter the playing area once the ball is played in that half. The coach can restrict that to be either the flank player passing the ball or the weakside flank player.
4. The coach may impose restrictions on where keepers must distribute the ball and what technique they must use.

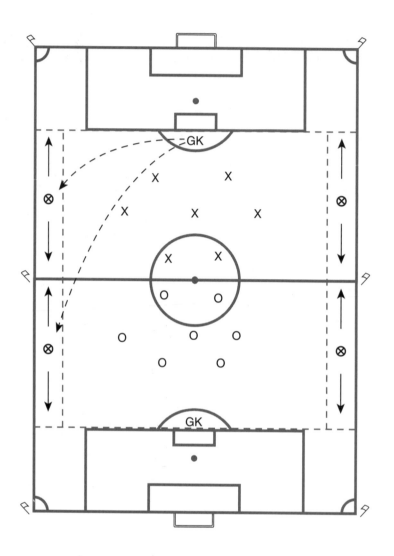

FULL-FIELD BUILD-UP

Team Exercise

Equipment   4 to 6 balls, disks, 2 regulation goals

Organization   Use disks to divide the field into thirds.

Procedure   Depending on your team's system of play, place defenders in the defending third of the field, midfielders in the midfield third of the field, and strikers in the attack third of the field. Place two defensive players in each third of the field, which creates an 11 v 6 situation. The coach starts the exercise by serving a ball to the goalkeeper, who must field the serve and initiate the attack by distributing to an appropriate player.

Training Tips   The coach should organize the proper pattern for the team as well as the type of build-up (direct, indirect, etc.) the team uses. As the team becomes more comfortable with their patterns and team shape, the coach may add more defenders and progress to an 11 v 11 situation.

Variations

1. The goalkeeper may initiate the attack only by throwing to the outside backs in the defending third of the field.
2. The goalkeeper may initiate the attack only by throwing to the outside midfielders in the midfield third of the field.
3. The goalkeeper may initiate the attack only by throwing or kicking to the strikers in the attack third of the field.
4. The exercise is started as a passback to the goalkeeper, who must control the ball with his or her feet and pass the ball to an open teammate. The same patterns and team shape described above apply, although the coach may want to emphasize a more direct attack when the ball is coming from the goalkeeper's feet.
5. Play unrestricted 11 v 11 except that the coach restarts any ball over the endline with a serve to the goalkeeper so that he or she may initiate the attack.

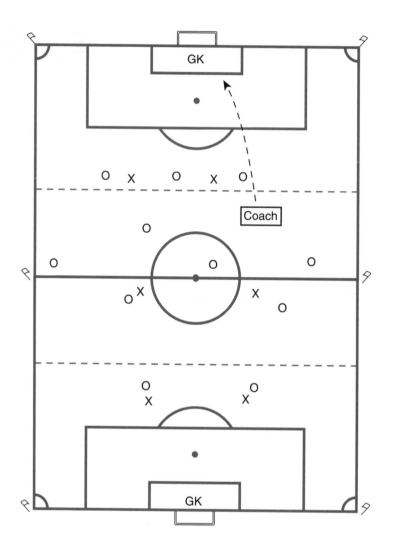

Organizing
the Defense

More than any other player on the team, the goalkeeper is in an excellent position to view the entire field. From a vantage point behind the defense, the keeper views the action as it develops and can communicate helpful information to the field players. Although excessive chatter is neither welcomed nor appropriate, verbal commands specific to the situation are valuable. Playing the role of "coach on the field" requires first and foremost that the keeper possess a thorough understanding of defensive tactics. What follows is a brief summary of the fundamental principles underlying group (area of the ball) and team defense. Goalkeeper communication with field players should reflect these principles. Commands should be delivered in a positive yet demanding manner, as there's little margin for error.

Fundamentals of Group Defense

The defending team is most vulnerable during the first few moments after a loss of possession. Players may be momentarily confused and disorganized as they switch from an attacking to defending mindset. To prevent a swift counterattack and possible opponent's score, defending players nearest the ball must initiate an immediate challenge to regain possession. Pressure at the point of attack is the foundation of solid team defense. It serves to delay immediate penetration of the defense via the pass or dribble and also stymies the opponent's efforts to initiate a swift counterattack. Immediate pressure at the point of attack also buys time for defending players positioned away from the ball to withdraw and regroup behind the ball.

Lack of pressure and failure to deny penetration of the defense are the most common reasons for conceding goals. The goalkeeper must be aware of this and, when necessary, remind teammates to "step up" to pressure the ball. The keeper should encourage teammates to keep play in front of the defense in order to prevent opponents from penetrating through open seams and into the vulnerable area behind the defense. This is accomplished through defensive principles called *pressure, cover*, and *balance.*

The defender positioned nearest the ball, referred to as the first (pressuring) defender, is responsible for providing immediate pressure at the point of attack. The pressuring defender must prevent the opponent with the ball from running at the defense and penetrating via the pass or dribble. The second (covering) defender has two primary responsibilities. The first is to control the space behind and to the side of the first defender. The covering defender must be in a position to intercept a pass slotted through that area and to step forward and challenge an opponent who has beaten the first defender on the dribble. The covering defender is also responsible for marking an opponent stationed in the immediate area of the ball. To fulfill both obligations, he or she must position at the correct angle and distance of cover. The third (balancing) defender positions in the space behind the second defender along an imaginary diagonal that begins at the ball and extends toward the goalpost farthest from the ball. From a position along the "line of balance," the third defender fulfills three important responsibilities: (1) protect the space behind the covering defender, (2) keep the ball in view at all times, and (3) keep the opponent he or she is marking in view (figure 12.1).

Fundamentals of Team Defense

The team's number one defensive priority is to limit the space and time available to opponents, particularly in the defending third of the field nearest their goal. To achieve this objective, consolidating players in the most dangerous scoring zones has become an accepted tactic. It's imperative that defending players, as a group, maintain the proper *defensive shape*. As defending players withdraw to a position behind (the goal side of) the ball, they should funnel inward toward the central area of the field. Positioning at the proper depth and angle of cover compacts the field horizontally, from side to side, and eliminates gaps of open space within the defense (figure 12.2).

As defending players withdraw and funnel inward, they must also provide cover, or support, for one another. This layering effect of players is sometimes called *vertical compactness*. The effect is to reduce space between defending players and ensure they don't align flat across the field.

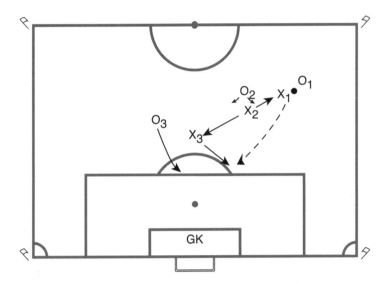

Figure 12.1 The line of balance. O_1 has the ball. X_1 is the first defender, applying direct pressure to the ball. O_2 is the supporting player. X_2 is the second defender or covering player. X_2 must mark O_2 but also be prepared to help X_1 in case O_1 beats X_1 on the dribble. X_3 provides balance, protecting the space behind X_1 and X_2. If O_1 tries to pass to O_3, X_3 should be in a position (goalside and inside) to cut off that pass. The line of balance is the line from X_1 to X_3.

Failure to achieve vertical compactness leaves a team vulnerable to passes slotted diagonally through the defense.

Measures must also be taken to protect the open space between the last line of defenders and the goalkeeper. A portion of this responsibility rests with the keeper, who should be prepared to sprint forward, outside of the penalty area if needed, to intercept passes slotted through the defense. Teammates help to control the space behind the defense by adhering to the principle of defensive balance. Players positioned on the side of the field opposite the ball withdraw to a position along an imaginary diagonal that begins at the ball and extends to the far post area of the goal. The greater the distance between a defending player and the ball, the deeper should be his or her position along the line of balance. The player should be able to keep the ball and the opponent he or she is marking in vision and also be able to cut off a long diagonal pass slotted into the space behind the defense.

Communication

Don't waste words! To avoid confusion, keepers' commands should be clear, concise, and to the point, following these basic guidelines:

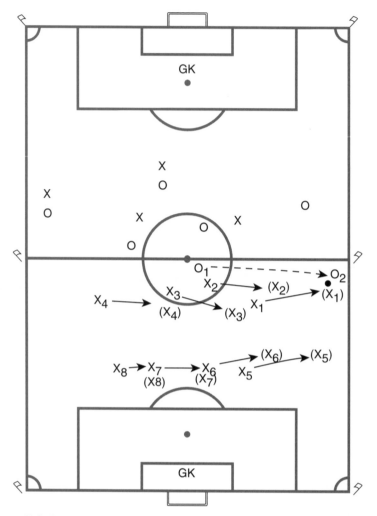

Figure 12.2 If O_1 has the ball, the Xs would maintain a compactness in the center of the field. If O_1 passes to O_2, the Xs would shift toward the ball and O_2. They would stay connected and horizontally compact, because once X_1 shifts to become the first defender, the entire team would then move with X_1. The parentheses indicate their new positions.

- **Keep it simple.** Commands should be purposeful and brief.
- **Be assertive.** Don't be shy about communicating useful information to teammates.
- **Call early.** Allow teammates ample time to respond.
- **Call loudly.** Urgency should be expressed in tone of voice. Usually there's not the luxury of repeating a command.

Most teams adopt a standard set of verbal commands to avoid confusion or misunderstanding among players. Common goalkeeper commands can be grouped into some general categories.

General Defensive Commands

These defensive commands are used to position teammates and organize the defense.

Call

- **"Mark-up!"** when you want a teammate to tightly mark an opponent.

- **"Close!" or "Step up!"** to instruct a teammate to apply greater pressure on an opponent with the ball.

- **"Help!"** to indicate that a player defending in a 1 v 1 situation needs cover.

- **"Weak side!"** to alert teammates to protect the space behind the defense opposite the position of the ball.

- **"Runner!"** to warn teammates that an opponent is making a blind-side run behind or through the defense. When possible, teammates should be informed of the direction of the run. For example, the keeper shouting, "John, right shoulder!" tells John that there's a player to his right who is out of his sight.

- **"Play to feet!"** when you want the ball passed back to you.

- **"Breakdown!" or "Stand him [or her] up!"** when you want a challenging defender to slow down and contain the attacker rather than diving in to tackle the ball.

Critical Defensive Commands

These commands are often used in situations where a moment of hesitation may prove costly. Commands must be decisive and issued without hesitation.

Shout

- **"Keeper!"** to let teammates (and opponents) know that you're moving into position to receive the ball.

- **"Away!"** when you want a teammate to immediately clear the ball first time away from the goalmouth.

General Attacking Commands

Although most communication involves defensive responsibilities, the keeper can also provide useful information once the team gets possession of the ball. These commands are used when the team is on attack.

Call

- **"Man-on!"** to warn a teammate that an opponent is closing down on him or her.

- **"Turn!" or "Time!"** to inform a teammate that he or she has sufficient space to turn with the ball to face the opponent's goal.

- **"Out!" or "Up!"** to order teammates out of the goal and penalty area after the ball has been cleared.

- **"Play wide!"** to let a teammate know that option is available to him or her.

Real Madrid's goalkeeper Dominguez Cesar directs his defenders during a game.

Organizing the Defense Drills

Verbal communication coupled with a fundamental understanding of defensive tactics is the key to organizing the defense. The exercises provided here are essentially suited for defenders, although the goalkeeper's role is crucial to successfully executing each drill. Verbal information provided by the keeper to field players enhances player awareness of the immediate situation and theoretically leads to improved decision making. With respect to the goalkeeper, the primary focus of the following drills should be on *what* is being communicated and *how* it is being communicated. Regular exposure to these situations will give the goalkeeper better understanding of what to say and when. The keeper will learn to issue commands earlier, more consistently, and more concisely.

INDIVIDUAL DEFENDING

Individual Exercise

Equipment 1 regulation goal, disks, 4 to 6 balls

Organization Mark a central channel the width of the goal area. An attacking player with the ball should be about 30 yards out, facing the goal. A defender is stationed on the endline next to the goal.

Procedure Play 1 v 1 to goal. When the attacking player dribbles forward, the defender sprints forward to close down the attacker and win the ball. The goalkeeper must disseminate important information to the defender on how to defend against the attacker.

Training Tips The goalkeeper's role is primarily providing verbal commands to the defender. Some suggestions:

1. "Close"—The first command the keeper must provide is for the defender to close down the ball. The goalkeeper's tone of voice should reflect the danger of the situation. For this exercise, the command should be loud and assertive, as the attacker is already in shooting range.

2. "Breakdown"—The keeper must remind the defender to break down into a good defensive posture so he or she can react to any move by the attacker and the defender is prepared to tackle the ball. The defender does not want to be running out of control, where there is a great tendency to "dive-in" for the ball. Experienced attackers can take advantage of this, and it is the keeper's job to remind the defenders.

3. "No foul"—This is crucial information, especially near the penalty area. Remind defenders to maintain composure.

4. "Force left/right"—The goalkeeper has a better view of the attacker's angle to goal, as well as the position of any covering defenders. This information can take away the attacker's shooting angle.

5. "No turn"—If the defender can force an attacker to turn his or her back to the goal, the defender needs to be reminded that the situation is no longer desperate and he or she needs to maintain patience to prevent a shot.

The goalkeeper also needs to constantly reposition based on the position of the first defender.

Variations

1. The defender starts even with the attacker and now must recover goalside before attempting to win the ball.

2. Place a server on the endline just outside the goal area. The defender is positioned in front of the goal. The attacker still starts from the same position but makes a run to the goal. The server attempts to play the ball to the attacker in the air or on the ground. *The defender must now maintain a position between the ball and the attacker.*

The keeper should communicate two additional crucial commands:

   a. "Right/left shoulder"—This lets the defender know an attacker is on an outside shoulder, so he or she can open the body to keep the attacker in view, preventing the attacker from being first to the ball.
   b. "Away" or "keeper"—This lets the defender know that he or she should clear the serve or that the goalkeeper can field it.

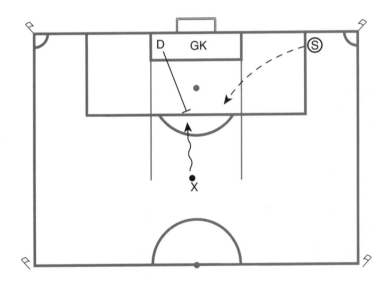

DEFENDING CROSSES

Group Exercise

Equipment 1 regulation goal, 6 to 8 balls

Organization Place two servers on each flank with a supply of balls. Place two defenders in the penalty area in front of the goal. Two attackers should be stationed 25 to 30 yards out, facing the goal.

Procedure The attackers make their runs to the goal. The defenders pick up the attackers as they make their runs into the box. The keeper or the defenders attempt to control or clear the ball, while the attackers try to score. Alternate serves from each flank.

Training Tips Defenders should open their bodies to keep the attackers and the ball in view, maintain a position between the ball and the attacker, and not allow the attacker to be first to the ball. The keeper should communicate the commands for crosses:

1. "Right/left shoulder"—This lets the defender know an attacker is on an outside shoulder.
2. "Away" or "keeper"—This lets the defender know that he or she should clear the serve or that the goalkeeper can field it.

If the attacker is able to receive the ball, commands for individual defending should be employed. The goalkeeper also needs to be constantly repositioning based on the position of the defenders and the runs of the attackers.

Variations

1. Add a third attacker so that the defenders and the keeper must decide who is most dangerous and who should be picked up.
2. Place the defenders and the servers even with the attackers. One of the attackers plays a ball into space for the server. The server chases down the pass and delivers a cross. The defenders now must recover and track the attackers.
3. Build up the number of the attackers and defenders, 3 v 2, 3 v 3, 4 v 3, to 6 v 4.

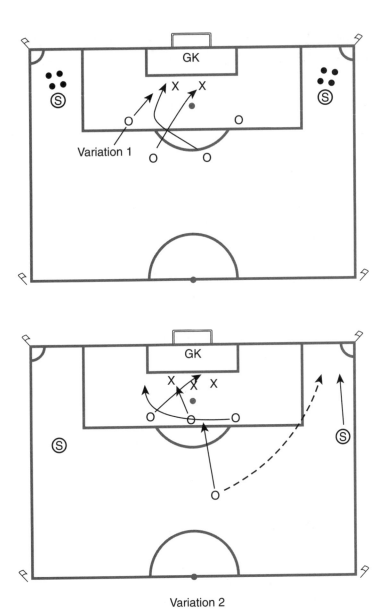

Variation 1

Variation 2

ORGANIZING THE BACK FOUR

Group Exercise

Equipment   1 regulation goal, disks, 6 to 8 balls

Organization   Play in half the field and divide it vertically into three equal sections. Place two attackers in the outside sections and three attackers in the center section, all near midfield. Organize four defenders 25 to 30 yards in front of the goal. A defender should be stationed in each outside channel, and two defenders should be stationed in the center section.

Procedure   Play in only one section at a time. In the outside channels there would be a 2 v 1 situation to goal, and in the center a 3 v 2. The attacking players on the flank may cut into the goal once they penetrate the edge of the penalty area. When that occurs, one of the central defenders should step in as a second, or covering, defender.

Training Tips   It is the goalkeeper's job to communicate with the defenders. The keeper should give the first defender pertinent commands for individual defending but also let the second defender know his or her role in providing cover. In addition to the aforementioned commands for individual defending and defending crosses, two other commands help when organizing a group of defenders.

1. "Delay"—This lets the first defender know he or she should not commit to tackle until the second defender arrives in a good covering position.
2. "Slide left/right"—This indicates to the second defender that he or she should slide toward the first defender to provide help and cover.
3. "Stay connected"—This informs a group of defenders that they cannot allow large gaps between each other and should stay connected, so proper shape (i.e., cover and balance) is maintained.

Variations

1. Play in two sections at once, with the second group not entering play until the ball is played into the second area. For example, if a flank player passes to a player in the center section, it would become a 5 v 3 in two-thirds of the field. The goalkeeper should provide information to those three defenders on when to pressure the ball and when to provide cover. All of the other previous commands still apply.
2. Still play two sections at a time, but now the ball is played to the opposite flank. For example, the ball starts on the right flank and goes to the center section and is then played to the left flank. This brings in the left side but puts those on the right side out of the game. This

situation also forces the fourth defender, the weakside defender, to stay connected with the two center backs. The goalkeeper now must be sure to communicate to the weakside defender to "tuck-in" from the other side of the field and stay connected although they were not originally in the play.

3. Use all three sections of the field and play 6 v 4 or 7 v 4 to goal. Use markers as guides only. The goalkeeper keys on maintaining a good playing shape for the back four defenders through proper communication and positioning.

4. Same as variation 3, but this time the back four defenders step up to midfield and play the attackers offside. This forces defenders to defend vertically as well as horizontally. The goalkeeper must now command defenders to "get out" of the back or "step up" to squeeze the space in the midfield. The keeper needs to be the impetus to get the defenders moving up the field.

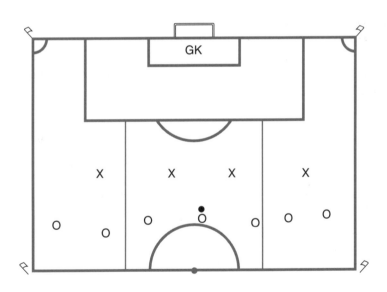

TEAM DEFENDING

Team Exercise

Equipment   1 regulation goal, flags, 6 to 8 balls

Organization   Play 11 v 8 in two-thirds of the field. Set up three small goals, three to four yards apart, using flags or, if available, small goals. The defenders are organized either four in the back and four in the midfield or three in the back and five in the midfield. The attacking team is organized in whatever system the coach deems appropriate.

Procedure   The coach restarts each play with a pass into a different area, which forces defenders to adjust their positions accordingly. If defenders win the ball, they attack one of the three small goals.

Training Tips   The main responsibility of the goalkeeper is to communicate to the defenders, so that a realistic team shape is maintained. All the previous commands apply for individual, group, and team defending. In addition, the goalkeeper must be sure to position correctly and stay focused on the ball.

The coach varies the type of pass and the location, intentionally playing into areas that might be vulnerable.

Variations

1. Restrict amount of touches for the defenders.
2. Give each defender a number, 1 to 8. Call out a number, and that defender kneels down and is out of the play, which creates an 11 v 7 situation. The goalkeeper and the defenders immediately react to the situation and adjust positions.
3. Same as variation 2, but put two defenders out of the play.

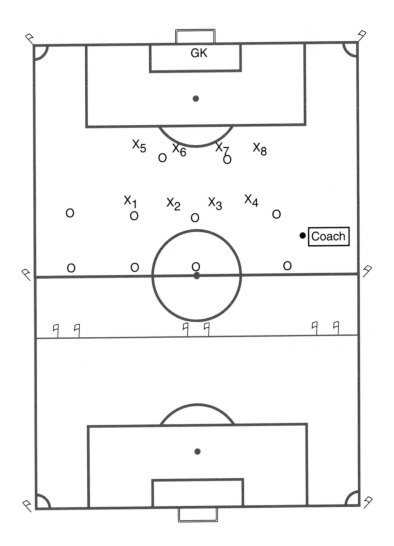

Index

About the Authors

Joe Luxbacher has more than 30 years of experience playing and coaching soccer at all levels. A former professional soccer player for the North American Soccer League, American Soccer League, and Major Indoor Soccer League, Luxbacher is the head coach of men's soccer at the University of Pittsburgh, a position he has held since 1984.

Luxbacher was named Big East Athletic Conference Coach of the Year in 1992 and 1995, and he was selected for the Beadling Soccer Club Hall of Fame in 1995. Luxbacher earned his PhD from the University of Pittsburgh in 1985 with specializations in physical education and management as well as administration of athletics. He lives in Pittsburgh, Pennsylvania.

The National Soccer Coaches Association of America honored **Gene Klein** as the 1996 National High School Coach of the Year. He has more than 30 years of playing and coaching experience, including a boys' high school team at Quaker Valley High School in Pennsylvania that claimed six state championships. He has served three seasons as an assistant coach for the Pittsburgh Riverhounds and spent over 10 years as the director of coaching for the Pennsylvania West Soccer Association. He is also a member of the coaching staff for U.S. Soccer Region 1 Boys' Olympic Development Program. A former goalkeeper, he has coached goalkeepers at the youth, high school, college, and pro levels.